WILLIAMSBURG RESEARCH STUDIES

WILLIAMSBURG RESEARCH STUDIES

Jane Carson
Colonial Virginia Cookery

Jane Carson
Colonial Virginians at Play

Jane Carson
James Innes and His Brothers of the F. H. C.

Jane Carson
Travelers in Tidewater Virginia: A Bibliography

Jane Carson
We Were There: Descriptions of Williamsburg

Hugh F. Rankin
Criminal Trial Proceedings in the General Court of Colonial Virginia

C. Clement Samford and John M. Hemphill II
Bookbinding in Colonial Virginia

James H. Soltow
The Economic Role of Eighteenth-Century Williamsburg

Thad W. Tate, Jr.
The Negro in Eighteenth-Century Williamsburg

COLONIAL VIRGINIA COOKERY

Colonial Virginia Cookery

By

JANE CARSON

Drawings by Ellen Eames

COLONIAL WILLIAMSBURG
Williamsburg, Virginia

Distributed by
THE UNIVERSITY PRESS OF VIRGINIA
Charlottesville

Printed in the United States of America

FOREWORD

WILLIAMSBURG RESEARCH STUDIES is a series of
specialized reports prepared as part of the research
program of Colonial Williamsburg. For forty years this
program has sought to fulfill a dual objective: to
supply the day-to-day information essential to the ac-
curate preservation and restoration of Williamsburg and
to supplement the interpretation of this colonial capital
with studies broad in scope and detailed in content. The
series makes available in inexpensive form the studies
of widest interest to students of the era and locality.

Since the series was inaugurated in 1965 with
the publication of seven selected reports from the files
of the Research Department, we have added an eighth report, Bookbinding in Colonial Virginia. The present
study, the ninth in the series, interprets the kitchens
in Williamsburg which are exhibited to the public.

The pieces of equipment drawn by Miss Eames
are all in the collections of Colonial Williamsburg.
Our research library contains the printed cookbooks,
English and American, on which the study was based.

The manuscript cookbook of Mrs. John Custis is owned
by the Historical Society of Pennsylvania, to whose
director, Mr. Nicholas B. Wainwright, we are grateful
for permission to use the manuscript.

Edward M. Riley
Director of Research

CONTENTS

INTRODUCTION

Like the English ladies of the eighteenth century who rushed into print with yet another cookbook, I feel that I owe the reader an explanation of my temerity. With Mrs. Smith I realize that "There are indeed already in the World Books that treat on this Subject, and which bear great Names," but with Mrs. Glasse "I Believe I have attempted a branch of cookery, which nobody has yet thought worth their while to write about."

Editors of old cookbooks and authors of books about colonial cookery are usually interested in reproducing the colonial dishes as nearly as possible; they address their books to modern cooks who want to prepare the old dishes in their own kitchens. The edited recipes accordingly are adapted to modern measurements, ingredients, and equipment, and offer few hints about colonial cooking methods. Readers interested in learning how colonial housewives managed to serve the elaborate meals that tradition ascribes to them must consult the historical sources. Collectors of antique cooking equipment, too, want to know how all the pieces were used and how to arrange them in a working colonial kitchen. It is to these cooks and

collectors that I address my study of the procedures in
colonial cooking.

For information about popular menus and dishes and
the food supplies available to Virginia housewives, I con-
sulted the conventional sources--letters and diaries, descriptions of natural resources, and books on gardening.
Travelers often praised the quality and quantity of Virginia food and drink and commented on local differences
from customs at home and in other parts of America; they
sometimes mentioned special dishes which appealed to them
or displeased them, but they never wrote out the complete
menu at any meal. Virginia diarists often recorded many
details about their farming operations--the weather, the
condition of crops and orchards and livestock--but no
housewife's diary has survived, and she, after all, was
the manager of the kitchen garden, the poultry yard, and
the dairy. Letters, too, yield only infrequent comments
on the concerns of the mistress of the household.

The letters of planters who were also enthusiastic
gardeners do contain useful information about their
success in growing European plants in the colony. The
author of the earliest American book on kitchen gardening--
John Randolph, the Tory--lived in Williamsburg; presumably
it was here that he made the experiments in adapting
English methods to Virginia gardens which he recorded as

A Treatise on Gardening by a Citizen of Virginia. No copy
of the first edition is known today, nor is there a record
of the date of publication; from internal evidence, however,
it is clear that Randolph wrote the book in the decade of
the 1760's after spending a number of years as a practicing
gardener. Jefferson's writings, so informative about almost every human activity, are especially interesting to
other gardeners and epicures, who may find in Thomas Jefferson's Garden Book, 1766-1824 pertinent comment on every
garden plant known in Virginia. Yet even Jefferson does not
answer all questions as precisely as one might wish. About
the tomato, for example, he tells us in 1782 that it was
common in Virginia gardens; he could buy it in the Washington markets all during his presidency; he did not grow
it at Monticello until 1809 but thereafter planted it regularly in several varieties.

For direct evidence of pieces of equipment in common
use in Virginia kitchens I examined orders for household
goods addressed to British merchants, newspaper advertisements of Virginia merchants, and the appraised inventories
of estates entered in county records. I found copies of
orders for utensils and supplies distressingly rare because the order was customarily sent as an enclosure,
which was not often copied into the writer's letter book
or preserved in his correspondence file. In this category

the Papers of John Norton and Sons, merchants of London and Virginia (Colonial Williamsburg Archives) are almost unique, for the collection contains recipients' copies of the letters, including enclosures. For advertisements of Virginia merchants I used the file of extant copies of Virginia Gazettes published in Williamsburg from 1736 to 1780.

Appraised inventories are so numerous that I could attempt only partial coverage. Through the years members of the Research Department of Colonial Williamsburg have been combing the York County records for data about Williamsburg people, buildings, and businesses; this file includes many inventories. Other files assembled by my colleagues for various economic studies contain inventories of estates and wills probated in courts all over the colony. In my own file of data concerning colonial women there are about 300 inventories of widows' estates, selected as representative of different levels of society and different areas of the colony. Valuable as all these lists are, they have serious limitations. They are not often complete because, by definition, personalty included only movable property and therefore any equipment built in or fastened down was excluded. Articles disposed of by will were usually removed before the inventory was made; if they were still in the house, the appraisers either ignored

them or entered them under the label "legacy" and did not
appraise them. The widow's third of her deceased husband's
estate was handled separately in a similar fashion.

Other conditions under which inventories were taken
affect their utility for my purposes. Household articles
were apparently assembled in groups for the attention of
the appraisers without reference to their normal place in
the house. It is helpful when the list is arranged by
rooms, but even when the kitchen was appraised separately,
articles from other outbuildings were often assembled there
for the inventory. The tendency of appraisers to value
metallic articles by weight makes entries of so many pounds
of pewter, iron, or brass of little use in determining the
popularity of specific cooking utensils. Finally, as one
would expect, the nomenclature used by individual appraisers
varied considerably according to his own familiarity with
kitchen utensils and the common names for them in his neigh-
borhood; this variation is especially noticeable in the identification of unfamiliar luxuries owned by great planters.

For information about cooking methods I have studied
the cookbooks that Virginia housewives owned and presumably
used. The obvious practical question of how written directions were followed in kitchens where illiterate servants
did the cooking was answered for me by an aged Monticello
slave named Isaac. When he was interviewed in the 1840's,

he recalled that during his childhood his mother was the pastry cook and that "Mrs. Jefferson would come out there with a cookery book in her hand & read out of it to Isaac's mother how to make cakes tarts & so on." From inventories, orders, advertisements, and ledgers I have been able to assemble a list of popular titles and to identify most of them. Identification is often difficult because of the universal habit of giving the title as it appeared on the spine of the book--never from the title page. Furthermore, the bookbinder's predilection for short titles compounds the difficulty with eighteenth-century cookbooks, which were as much alike in title as in content. "Bradley's Housewife" in 1772, for example, may be an old copy of The Country Housewife and Lady's Director by Richard Bradley (first edition 1727 with later reprints) or a new copy of The British Housewife: or, the Cook, Housekeeper's and Gardiner's Companion by Mrs. Martha Bradley (first edition c. 1770); or it may be a book unknown to me.

The number of modern collectors who specialize in old cookbooks has produced several good bibliographical aids to identification. In addition to catalogues of the British Museum and the Library of Congress, I have used Arnold W. Oxford, English Cookery Books to the Year 1850 (Oxford University Press, 1913); Waldo Lincoln, American Cookery Books 1742-1860 (American Antiquarian Society, revised edition 1954); W. Carew Hazlitt, Old Cookery Books and Ancient Cuisine (London, 1902); Elizabeth R. Pennell, My Cookery Books (Boston, 1903); Esther B. Aresty, The Delectable Past (New York, 1964).

The most popular English cookbooks in Virginia were Mrs. Smith's, Mrs. Glasse's, Mrs. Harrison's, Mrs. Raffald's, and Mrs. Bradley's. While this general statement may be made with confidence, it is not often possible to say precisely what titles a given person owned at a given time. Take the case of John Mercer of Marlborough. When he made a catalogue of his books in 1746, he owned "May's Cookery" in octavo. Among the books he had purchased from Robert Beverley in 1730 was "The Accomplished Cook"--the same book: Robert May, The Accomplisht Cook, Or the Art and Mystery of Cookery (first edition London, 1660). When his library was sold after his death, it did not include a copy of May; instead there were [Richard] "Bradley's Country Housewife," [E. Smith's] "Complete Housewife," and [John Evelyn's] "Discourse on Sallads" [Acetaria, A Discourse on Sallets, first edition 1699]. All this is understandable, but what happened to the copy of Mrs. Glasse that he bought at the Virginia Gazette Office on April 11, 1764?

The first edition of E. Smith, The Compleat Housewife; or, Accomplished Gentlewoman's Companion was published in London in 1727; other London editions came out in 1728,

1729, 1730, 1732, 1734, 1736, 1739, 1741, 1742, and on
through the century, with the eighteenth edition in 1773.
Mrs. Smith's book was one of a series which began to appear at the end of the seventeenth century, written by
women from their own experience as housekeepers in fashionable English families. Their predecessors had been
men serving "Kings, Princes, and Noblemen," either French-
men, or Englishmen who could boast of a French apprentice-
ship. Robert May, for example, after thorough training in
France and fifty years of successful attendance on persons
of honour in England, had felt compelled to reveal the
whole art and mystery of cookery because "God and My Con-
science would not permit me to bury these my Experiences in
the Grave." Mrs. Smith in her preface modestly disclaimed
all pretense to literary merit or exotic diversity in favor
of brevity, frugality, and practicality, promising "Directions generally for dressing after the best, most natural
and wholesome Manner, such Provisions as are the Product
of our own Country, and in such a Manner as is most agreeable to English Palates." During thirty years of constant
employment in "fashionable and noble" houses, she collected
and tested the recipes that she now presented in a business-
like manner. While omitting the customary moral maxims and
essays on Christian duty along with the "whimsical," the
"impracticable," and "the odd and fantastical Messes" in

larger collections, she did not hesitate to borrow recipes freely from her predecessors. Nor in the selection and arrangement of her recipes is her book a complete departure from earlier medleys; of her 800 recipes, 300 are for medicines and salves and about 100 for cordial waters and cosmetics.

E. Smith has not been identified; all that we know of her we learn from her book. The fifth edition (London, 1732) mentioned her "recent" death, probably in 1731. It was this fifth edition that William Parks reprinted in 1742 for sale in his Williamsburg Printing Office--the first known cookbook published in British America. So that he might reduce the price of the book from five shillings to four, he reduced its size by using smaller pages with narrower margins, smaller type, and fewer recipes. He explained in his preface that he had omitted "Recipes, the Ingredients or Materials for which, are not to be had in this Country." But a comparison of his text with the London edition shows that ingredients for many of his omissions were plentiful in Virginia and suggests that he used his personal taste as a guide and left out dishes that did not appeal to him. While he retained Mrs. Smith's language and spelling, he changed the London printer's punctuation and capitalization to conform with his own style.

Apparently Parks's edition sold well. It was

reprinted in 1752 by his successor, William Hunter, who advertised it in May as "just published" under the title The Compleat Housewife; or, Accomplish'd Gentlewoman's Companion and bound with Every Man His Own Doctor. The recipes, Hunter explained, were collected from the sixth edition (London, 1734). I have not been able to compare Hunter's text with others because no copy of his imprint has been located.

Again, in 1775 and 1776, Mrs. Smith's Complete House Wife was advertised for sale in Williamsburg when John Dixon and William Hunter, Jr., included it in their lists of octavos without reference to the edition available at that time. The different spelling and capitalization, together with the casual listing, suggest that these copies had just come in from London, where the book was still being reprinted every few years.

Another cookbook sold at the Gazette Office in the 1760's and 1770's was The House-keeper's Pocket-book, and Compleat Family Cook: Containing Above Twelve Hundred Curious and Uncommon Receipts in Cookery, Pastry, Preserving, Pickling, Candying, Collaring, &c. with Plain and easy Instructions for Preparing and Dressing every Thing suitable for an Elegant Entertainment, from Two Dishes to Five or Ten, &c. and Directions for ranging them in their proper Order...by Mrs. Sarah Harrison, of Devonshire

(first edition London, 1733, with revisions and reprints
through a ninth edition, 1777). Our copy in the Research
Library is the sixth, 1755.

Mrs. Harrison's special forte was a combination of
broad subject coverage, care for economy, and the brevity
implied in her Pocket-book designation. In the sixth edition she crowded the 1200 recipes into 215 duodecimo pages
and added a new section of thirty-six pages under the subtitle Every one their own Physician; A Collection of the
most approved Receipts for the Cure of most Disorders inci-
dent to Human Bodies. As a further aid to housewives she included arithmetical tables of interest rates and relative
values of coins. The bill of fare featured in her title she
carefully defined: an "admirable Contrivance, to supply,
at one View, the frugal Mistress of a Family with a perfect
Knowledge of every Thing that is in Season; so that she
has nothing more to do than to select what is fittest for
the Table."

After dedicating her vade mecum "to all the good
housewives in Great-Britain," she prepared for them a sort
of credo on the importance of cookery and good household
management. "Certainly," she declared, "no Art whatsoever,
relating to terrestrial Things, ought to claim a Preference
to that which makes Life easy." In her opinion elegance
might be achieved without extravagance: "A few good

Ingredients make the best Dishes, and a Crowd of rich
Things are apter to satiate, than to please the Palates
of those who have the nicest Taste." Her very brief recipes, therefore, name all the necessary ingredients but
seldom include cooking instructions or suggest elaborate
garnishes.

The best-seller among eighteenth-century cookbooks and
the best known today was first published in London in 1747
as The Art of Cookery Made Plain and Easy...By a Lady; it
was reissued steadily into the nineteenth century, with
two Virginia editions published in Alexandria in 1805 and
1812. "Mrs. Glasse's Cookery" also appears more frequently
than any other cookbook in Virginia inventories, and it was
advertised more often in the Virginia Gazettes of the 1760's
and 1770's. Furthermore, the fragmentary Virginia Gazette
Day Books record sales throughout the years 1764-1766.

The standard explanation of its sales record is that
the mystery surrounding its authorship invited titillative
speculation and increased its interest as a possible literary hoax. There are now few discoverable facts. The
first three editions carried no hint of authorship. In
the fourth edition (1751) the autograph H. Glasse was en-
graved in the conventional way at the top of the first
page of the text, but the title page continued to read
"By a Lady." Then in the decade of the 1760's, at the

height of the book's popularity, two new publications

appeared: <u>The Complete Confectioner...By H. Glasse, Author</u>

<u>of the Art of Cookery</u> and <u>The Servant's Directory...By H.</u>

<u>Glasse, Author of The Art of Cookery</u>. At that time it

was widely believed in London that the author was a Fleet

Street hack writer--Dr. John Hill or another--and bibliog-

raphers and bibliophiles still argue the question whether

Mrs. Glasse ever existed.

In my opinion, the possibility that "H. Glasse" was

a pseudonym did not affect the value of the cookbook. It

is reasonable to suppose that colonial Virginians bought

it for its practical cooking instructions, because they

planned to use it--not because they collected literary

hoaxes. The extant inventories of their libraries reveal

no interest in literary curiosities, and of all the sur-

viving examples of the cookbooks available to them before

1770, it is the best.

Believing that "every servant who can but read will

be capable of making a tolerable good cook," Mrs. Glasse

avoided the conventional "high polite stile" and wrote her

instructions for the persons who actually did the cooking.

She was not trying to "direct a lady in the oeconomy of

her family" or to give medical advice. Yet she would serve

the interests of the mistress of the household by fore-

stalling the kind of extravagance associated with French

chefs, who used six pounds of butter to fry twelve eggs
"when every body knows (that understands cooking) that
half a pound is full enough." She did not expect to
please English gentlemen who "would rather be imposed on
by a French booby, than give encouragement to a good English cook" but hoped to "improve the servants, and save
the ladies a great deal of trouble."

There is no question of the reality of Mrs. Raffald,
author of The Experienced English House-keeper, for the
Use and Ease of Ladies, House-keepers, Cooks, &c. (first
edition Manchester, 1769; later editions to the twelfth
[1799] published in various places, usually London). She
was born Elizabeth Whitaker in Doncaster, Yorkshire, 1733,
and as a young woman served for fifteen years in several
county families. In 1763 she was housekeeper to the Hon.
Lady Elizabeth Warburton of Arley Hall, Cheshire, when
she married the Arley Hall gardener, John Raffald. The
couple moved to Manchester, where she spent the remaining
eighteen years of her busy life. She was the mother of
sixteen daughters. She was the proprietor of a successful
confectionery shop and manager of several inns. She opened
a registry office for domestic servants. She conducted a
school of cookery and domestic economy for young ladies.
She compiled several city directories and contributed articles to two newspapers. When she died, in 1781, she had

almost finished writing a book on midwifery.

Like Fanny Burney a decade later, Mrs. Raffald

feared the contempt of critics because her cookbook was

written by a woman:

> When I reflect upon the number of books
> already in print upon this subject, and with
> what contempt they are read, I cannot but be
> apprehensive, that this may meet with the
> same fate from some, who will censure it be-
> fore they either see it or try its value.

But like Mrs. Glasse three decades earlier, she expected

women to value her recipes; she had written them in a plain

style and "purely from practice," then tested them and

proofread them with painstaking care. Her aim was "to

please both the eye and the palate" without extravagance--

"to join economy with neatness and elegance."

Her book was an immediate success. Though it was

first published "for the author" in Manchester, where her

reputation and connections would ensure good sales, copies

were distributed to booksellers all over England. In her

advertising she did not neglect to mention other business

enterprises. She guaranteed her confectionery recipes to

be "such as I daily sell in my own shop." Her announce-

ments in The Manchester Mercury and Harrop's General Ad-

vertiser closed with the thanks of John and Elizabeth

Raffald for past favors, a notice of recent additions and

improvements at their inn, and the assurance that "Neat

post chaises with able horses and careful drivers may be had at the inn on the shortest notice."

Since booksellers in the colonies did not receive the attention accorded Londoners, they did not often stock brand-new publications. Partly for this reason, no doubt, Williamsburg newspapers did not advertise Mrs. Raffald's book. But Hannah (Lee) Corbin bought a copy in June of 1772, and other Virginians owned the book before the Revolution.

A contemporary of Mrs. Raffald--Mrs. Bradley--returned to the seventeenth-century style for her two-volume manual, The British Housewife: or, the Cook, Housekeeper's and Gardiner's Companion...By Mrs. Martha Bradley, late of Bath: being the Result of upwards of Thirty Years Experience (London, [c.1770?]), which was for sale in Williamsburg as early as 1771. She arranged her instructions by months, and so the book is divided into twelve parts. Each part devotes much attention to marketing efficiency and the planning of menus in town and country, and there is a section each month on the management of cattle and poultry, garden and orchard. The common diseases of family and livestock are diagnosed each month and remedies suggested. Discussions of other problems of household management are scattered through the book: fashions in food service and table manners, instructions for trussing game in the kitchen and for carving it at table, suggestions for wedding suppers and other special occasions.

Anticipating the reader's difficulties in using a book of such broad "Scope and Compass," Mrs. Bradley explained her method of presentation. In the January section she gave "such Directions...as shall alone be sufficient for the general Information of the Housekeeper, or Mistress of a Family, and Instruction of the common Servant," leaving the more "difficult and elegant Particulars" of interest to her more accomplished readers for "succeeding Numbers." In spite of her "great Care" the public apparently did "construe" her arrangement to her "Disadvantage," for the book did not sell well enough to require new editions, and it is exceedingly rare in modern collections. The copy in the Research Library is incomplete after the first of October; we have only three of the four volumes in which it is bound. The frontispiece of our copy is an interesting bibliographical puzzle which illustrates the amount of borrowing among compilers of the cookbooks of the period. It is labeled "Frontispiece to the Compleat English Cook," which is the title of a book published in 1762 under the authorship of "Catherine Brooks of Red-Lyon-Street." After the death of Mrs. Raffald, Mrs. Brooks in her turn borrowed Mrs.

Raffald's old title when she brought out a new edition in Manchester, instead of London.

Virginia cookbooks in manuscript that have survived from colonial times are hard to find, though nineteenth-century ones are plentiful. I have examined only one that I am sure was compiled early in the eighteenth century-- a collection of recipes assembled by Frances (Parke) Custis and now owned by the Historical Society of Pennsylvania. Marie Kimball edited it for publication in 1940 and called it The Martha Washington Cook Book because Martha owned it until she gave it to Nelly Custis. It is a small leather-bound volume in good condition, and the handwriting is beautiful and legible. The recipes are arranged in two parts: A Booke of Cookery containing 206 entries and A Booke of Sweetmeats containing 326. Each part has a table of contents written in the same hand.

The even spacing and paragraphing on each page, the regularity of the penmanship throughout the volume, and the systematic arrangement of recipes suggest that the collection was made over a short period of time. I am unable to make an intelligent guess about the date of compilation because sources are not cited and I do not recognize the recipes. They are all English; the ingredients and arrangement are conventional; the irregularities in spelling are not great enough to suggest that the recipes

were taken down from dictation. I conclude, therefore,
that Mrs. Custis copied them from a printed seventeenth-
century cookbook I have never seen. From the elegant tone
of the collection and the disproportionate size of the confectionery section, I infer that the compiler planned to
use it for "company" dishes in a program of elaborate entertainment. Knowing that the compiler was Mrs. John Custis,
I investigated her record as a housekeeper to find out
how well she used it.

Frances Parke and her sister Lucy are remembered today for high-spirited treatment of famous husbands, John
Custis and William Byrd. Their personal eccentricities
are usually attributed to their resemblance to their father,
Daniel Parke, whose behavior during the last years of his
life was bitterly resented by both sons-in-law because it
encumbered his estate with debts and litigation which
threatened them with bankruptcy. Both husbands recorded
opinions of the sisters as wives which have often been
quoted, but little has been said of them as housewives.

They grew up on their father's Queen's Creek plantation just outside Williamsburg. When Frances was eleven
years old, Parke went to England in search of political
preferment that would lead to the governor's office in
the colony. The quest kept him in the mother country year
after year, always promising his family an early return

under circumstances that would make them all "great and
happy." Their mother, managing his property without his
help and not doing it very efficiently, had to struggle
to keep up appearances, but she, too, taught her daughters
to live like gentlewomen.

Frances's husband was as well-to-do as Lucy's, if
not so attractive and good humored. They maintained two
households, his Arlington plantation on the Eastern Shore
as well as Queen's Creek, which Custis managed first at
Parke's request and then as his wife's inheritance. Byrd
always commented favorably on the warmth of his welcome
at Queen's Creek and never criticized the fare or the service. Arlington, however, was "not kept very nicely," the
servants the worst he ever saw in his life, the food monotonous, the wine "very scarce" and of inferior quality.
Apparently the Custis marital squabbles stemmed from dis-
agreements about living arrangements and finances. He
wanted to live at Arlington and thought her extravagant;
she preferred Queen's Creek and thought him stingy. Their
famous marriage agreement of 1714 supports this view. In
it he promised to allow her adequate household supplies
from the produce of the estate; wheat, corn, meat, cider,
and brandy were specifically mentioned. She in turn promised not to exceed her allowance or to interfere in his
business if he would not intermeddle in her domestic

affairs. The agreement was made too late to improve the housekeeping at Arlington, for Frances died of smallpox the following year.

The author of the first printed Southern cookbook, The Virginia Housewife: or, Methodical Cook by Mrs. Mary Randolph (Washington, 1824), was a Virginia housewife who was reputed to be the best cook in Richmond three decades earlier. Mary (Randolph) Randolph (1762-1828), a daughter of the elder Thomas Mann Randolph of Tuckahoe, married her cousin, David Meade Randolph. The young couple set up housekeeping in Richmond and became the center of a group of Federalists famous for wit and good fellowship. Their hospitable home was called "Moldavia" in tribute to the hosts, Molly and David. The election of 1800 cost Randolph his post as marshal of Virginia, and his violent anti-Jeffersonian sentiments prevented his future appointment to public office.

During years of increasing financial embarrassment, Moldavia was sold and Mrs. Randolph was the mistress of a series of boarding houses. She now enjoyed a new sobriquet, "the Queen," which originated in the excitement following a Negro insurrection planned for August 31, 1800. It was prevented because several slaves informed their masters in time to assemble the militia and capture the ring-leaders. Depositions taken at their trials gave conflicting accounts

of their aims, but most of them agreed that they planned
to set fire to the Capitol, the Penitentiary, and the Ar-
mory and draw all the men to that end of town, then to
take the city block by block and kill every white male
who opposed them. "General" Gabriel, the chief plotter,
was quoted as saying he would spare only one white person,
Mrs. David Meade Randolph, that he was going to save her
to be his queen because she knew so much about cooking.

A few years later another villain praised her somewhat extravagantly. Harman Blennerhassett, in Richmond
for Burr's trial, met her at a Federalist tea and found
her "a middle-aged lady, and very accomplished; of charm-
ing manners, and possessing a masculine mind" distinguished
by "acute penetration" and "informed judgment."

After the Burr fiasco Mrs. Randolph disappeared
from the Richmond scene. She died January 23, 1828, in
Washington, D.C., and was buried at Arlington. She had
apparently been living for some time in or near the George-
town home of a son, William Beverley Randolph. It was
here that she probably wrote the cookbook; it was published
in Washington, and her son William held the copyright on
the 1828 edition.

The Virginia Housewife enjoyed a long and active
life. A second edition was published in 1825, a third
in 1828, a fourth in 1830, and a fifth in 1831 in

stereotype, which was repeatedly reprinted in other cities--
Baltimore, Philadelphia, New York--into the twentieth century. The College of William and Mary owns a first edition,
the Virginia State Library a second, the Virginia Historical
Society a collection of nine early printings from 1830
through 1888; in the Research Library are a first edition
and a stereotype published in Philadelphia, 1855.

A detailed comparison of early editions shows that
revisions and additions were made by the author for the
second edition. Her only illustrations appear in this
edition alone: three engravings illustrating two of her
inventions. One is a bath, the other a refrigerator similar to the ice box that was still in common use when
electric refrigerators replaced it. Richmond tradition
states that a "shrewd Yankee" patron of her boarding
house saw the model she had constructed for her own use,
"carried the invention" home with him, and later patented
it.

Mrs. Randolph's brief preface and introduction ex-
pound her subtitle, "Method is the Soul of Management," in
terms of her own experience. "The difficulties I encount-
ered," she explained, "when I first entered on the duties
of a housekeeping life, from the want of books sufficiently
clear and concise to impart knowledge to a Tyro" had compelled her to work out her own methods and recipes "by

actual experiment." Her purpose in writing the book was

to provide a practical guide for young inexperienced

housekeepers whose needs were like her own so many years

earlier. I have used her recipes extensively in prepar-

ing this report because her statement that they were

"written from memory, where they were impressed by long

continued practice" guarantees them today as the best

culinary practice in her Virginia.

"The grand arcanum of management" she stated in

three simple rules: "Let every thing be done at a proper

time, keep every thing in its proper place, and put every

thing to its proper use." A good manager should begin

her day with an early breakfast, the whole family in

attendance together for a "social and comfortable" meal.

Then while the servants had breakfast in the kitchen,

she should employ herself "in washing the cups, glasses,

&c.; arranging the cruets, the mustard, salt-sellers,

pickle vases, and all the apparatus for the dinner table."

The kitchen breakfast over, she should "go in to give her

orders" and have "all the articles intended for the dinner,

pass in review before her: have the butter, sugar, flour,

meal, lard, given out in proper quantities; the catsup,

spice, wine, whatever may be wanted for each dish, meas-

ured to the cook."

This procedure would ensure economy and relieve the

mistress of "the horrible drudgery of keeping house all day, when one hour devoted to it in the morning, would release her from trouble until the next day." Taking a broader view of the housewife's duty, she concluded:

The prosperity and happiness of a family depend greatly on the order and regularity established in it. The husband, who can ask a friend to partake of his dinner in full confidence of finding his wife unruffled by the petty vexations attendant on the neglect of household duties--who can usher his guest into the dining-room assured of seeing that methodical nicety which is the essence of true elegance,--will feel pride and exultation in the possession of a companion, who gives to his home charms that gratify every wish of his soul, and render the haunts of dissipation hateful to him. The sons bred in such a family will be moral men, of steady habits; and the daughters, if the mother shall have performed the duties of a parent in the superintendence of their education, as faithfully as she has done those of a wife, will each be a treasure to her husband; and being formed on the model of an exemplary mother, will use the same means for securing the happiness of her own family, which she has seen successfully practiced under the paternal roof.

COLONIAL VIRGINIA COOKERY

I. PROVISIONS AND MENUS

The abundance and variety of the food in colonial Virginia evoked extravagant praise from everyone who commented on it. John Hammond, for example, in 1656 characterized Virginians as "affable, courteous and very assistant to strangers"--for, "what but plenty makes hospitality and good neighbourhood?"[1] He explained that:

> Cattle and Hogs are every where, which yeeld
> beef, veal, milk, butter, cheese and other
> made dishes, porke, bacon, and pigs, and that
> as sweet and savoury meat as the world affords,
> these with the help of Orchards and Gardens,
> Oysters, Fish, Fowle and Venison, certainly
> cannot but be sufficient for a good diet and
> wholsom accommodation, considering how plen-
> tifully they are, and how easie with industry
> to be had.[2]

At the end of the century, the Virginia historian Robert Beverley attempted to present a systematic listing of the native products customarily used for food. Trees yielded cherries, plums, mulberries, persimmons; chestnuts, hazelnuts, hickory nuts, walnuts; maple sugar.

---

1. John Hammond, <u>Leah and Rachel or, The Two Fruitfull Sisters Virginia, and Mary-land</u> (London, 1656) in Peter Force, ed., <u>Tracts and Other Papers</u> ... (Washington, 1836-1846), III, No. 14, p. 15.

2. <u>Ibid</u>., p. 13.

1

Wild shrubs produced cranberries, currants, huckleberries, raspberries; chinquapins. Strawberries and six varieties of wild grapes had been successfully transplanted into domestic gardens. Melons included several kinds of watermelons, muskmelons and macocks; also there were pumpkins, cymlings, yellow squash, four varieties of maize, potatoes both red and white, peas of several kinds, kidney beans, limas and others.[3]

"As for Fish," he continued, "both of Fresh and Salt-Water, of Shell-Fish, and others, no Country can boast of more Variety, greater Plenty, or of better in their several Kinds."[4] Among the varieties he himself had eaten he listed: bass, carp, cat, chub, drum, flounder, herring, mullet, needlefish, alewives, perch, pike, plaice, rock, shad, sheepshead, sturgeon, sunfish, taylor, trout, whiting; eels and lampreys; crabs, oysters, cockles and mussels, shrimp.[5]

About wildfowl he wrote:

> As in Summer, the Rivers and Creeks are fill'd with Fish, so in Winter they are in many Places cover'd with Fowl. There are such a Multitude of Swans, Geese, Brants, Sheldrakes,

---

3. Robert Beverley, The History and Present State of Virginia, ed. by Louis B. Wright (Chapel Hill, 1947), pp. 129-134, 136, 141-145.

4. Ibid., p. 146.

5. Ibid., p. 147.

Ducks of several Sorts, Mallard, Teal, Blew-
ings, and many other Kinds of Water-Fowl, that
the Plenty of them is incredible.... In like
manner are the Mill-Ponds, and great Runs in
the Woods stor'd with these Wild-Fowl, at cer-
tain Seasons of the Year.
  The Shores, Marshy Grounds, Swamps, and
Savanna's, are also stor'd with the like Plenty
of other Game, of all Sorts, as Cranes, Curlews,
Herons, Snipes, Woodcocks, Saurers, Ox-eyes,
Plover, Larks, and many other good Birds for
the Table that they have not yet found a Name
for.... [Inland they have] Wild Turkeys, of an
incredible Bigness, Pheasants, Partridges, Pigeons, and an Infinity of small Birds, as well
as Deer, Hairs, Foxes, Raccoons, Squirrels,
Possums.[6]

But the early colonists did not depend upon indige-

nous food supplies. The first group brought along English

grain for immediate sowing and each succeeding "supply"

fleet carried other stocks of seeds and animals. Of the

imported stock, swine fared best. "Hogs swarm like Ver-

mine upon the Earth," Beverley declared, because they

"run where they list, and find their own Support in the

Woods, without any Care of the Owner."[7] This way of life

produced the lean, razor-back hog whose flesh gave Vir-

ginia ham and bacon their distinctive flavor.[8]

Epicures found Virginia beef somewhat inferior

---

6. _Ibid._, p. 153.

7. _Ibid._, p. 318.

8. Philip Alexander Bruce, _Economic History of
Virginia in the Seventeenth Century_ (2 vols., New York,
1896), II, 198-199.

because cattle, raised like swine, were lean and tough after a winter in the woods, and even when they were penned and fed with grain before butchering, they never achieved the sleek fatness that made English beef so delicious.[9] Beverley deplored his countrymen's habit of starving young cattle and suggested that they drain the "noble Marshes" and "make as fine Pastures as any in the World."[10]

Goats, chickens, geese and other domestic fowls thrived like hogs. But sheep, imported quite early, were never so numerous, for Virginians ate venison instead of mutton.[11] In England the importance of the wool industry dictated the popularity of mutton; in the colony, however, briars and bushes damaged the fleeces of sheep grazing in the wilderness.

Transported flora, too, flourished here. Beverley boasted: "I don't know any English Plant, Grain, or Fruit, that miscarries in Virginia.... No Seed is Sowed ...but it thrives, and most Plants are improved by being Transplanted thither."[12] He praised the quality of

---

9. Ibid., p. 198.

10. Beverley, Virginia, pp. 291, 318.

11. Bruce, Economic History, II, 199.

12. Beverley, Virginia, pp. 293, 314.

apples, nectarines, apricots, and peaches that grew to twelve inches in circumference; European grapevines; almonds, pomegranates and figs; wheat, barley, oats, rye.[13] Though he had little personal interest in vegetables, he noticed in the kitchen gardens of his neighbors "all the Culinary Plants that grow in England."[14]

A generation later, when William Byrd II was trying to promote settlement of his back-country lands, he prepared a list of favorite vegetables and herbs in Virginia gardens: artichokes, asparagus, beans of many kinds, beets, broccoli, four kinds of cabbage, cauliflower, carrots, cress, cucumbers, several varieties of lettuce, mustard, onions, parsnips, potatoes, radishes, rhubarb, spinach, truffles, turnips; also chives, fennel, garlic, horse-radish, parsley, sorrel, angelica, anise, borage, burnet, coriander, dill, marjoram, rosemary, savory, yarrow and others.[15]

With this great wealth of provisions available in the colony,[16] only a few articles of food were regularly

---

13. Ibid., pp. 314-316.

14. Ibid., p. 292.

15. Richard C. Beatty and William J. Mulloy, William Byrd's Natural History of Virginia, or The Newly Discovered Eden (Richmond, 1940), pp. 22-23.

16. A Yorktown doctor boasted: "...Virginia is the

imported. Sugar was needed to supplement honey from wild or domestic hives and to replace maple sugar when a bland sweetening agent was desired. Only Lisbon or "bay" salt from southern Europe was suitable for curing meat. Conventional tastes required lavish use of spices; all but the poor, therefore, bought pepper, cloves, mace, cinnamon, ginger. Popular luxuries included oranges and lemons, raisins and prunes, packaged sweetmeats, European wines, English beer, West Indian rum. With all these supplies at hand, the Virginia housewife was prepared to set the most opulent of dinner tables.

If she wished to be fashionable as well, she had only to seek the guidance of her English cookbooks. Apparently the mistress of a great plantation did pay close attention to style, for European guests noted that her dishes were dressed in the English taste and served in the English fashion. In planning her menus she emphasized dinner, the main meal of the day, which she served at two or three o'clock in the afternoon. Her cookbooks dictated two courses, each carefully planned to give an appearance of ordered abundance symmetrically displayed.[17] The first

---

most Plentiful Country for Provisions in the known World." Matthew Pope to John Jacob, August 25, 1775, p. 2, Additional Manuscripts, 34813, British Museum. CW M-283.

17. Diagrams for her guidance were included in several of her cookbooks, and an elaborately complete guide was

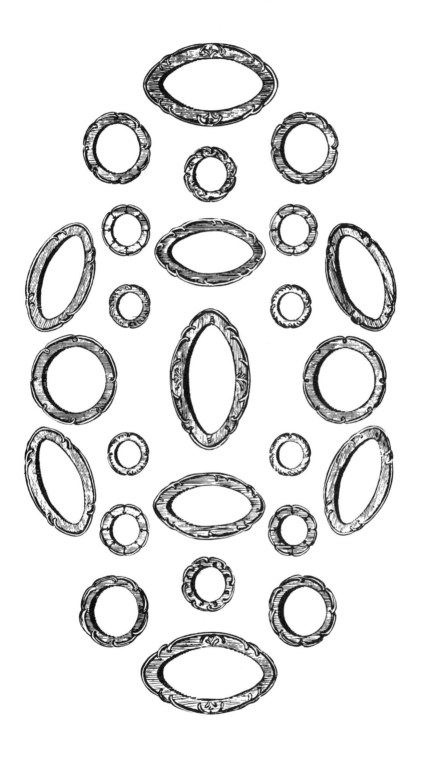

Mrs. Raffald's Plan of a Grand Table of Two Covers
First Course

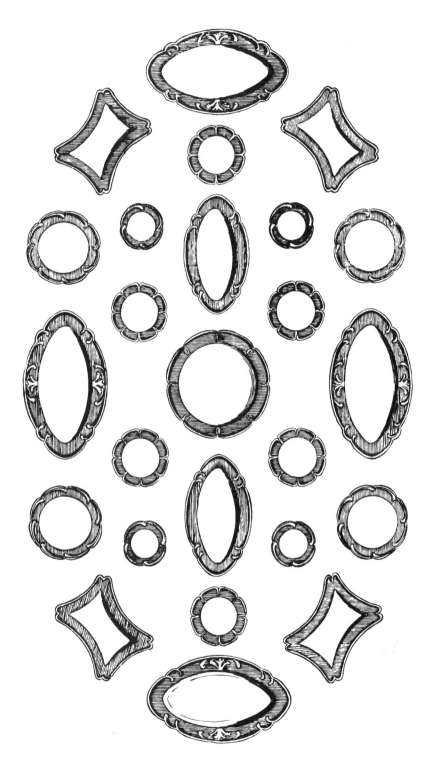

Mrs. Raffald's Plan of a Grand Table of Two Covers
Second Course

course featured large cuts of meat, whole fowls and fish--preferably boiled or baked--with supplementary meat dishes of almost any kind. The second was made up of smaller cuts of other meats and game birds, roasted, and seafood dishes surrounding a variety of desserts--puddings, pastries, jellies, sweetmeats. Soup was placed on the table as a first-course dish, served by the hostess and then replaced by a conventional meat or fish. Vegetables might appear in either course as garnishes or complements of meat dishes. Also suitable for either course were meat and seafood pies or made dishes of mixed ingredients.

There were conventions about the progression of dishes, which Mrs. Harrison stated as rules:

> It is to be observed, that, in the Course of Dinners, the grosser Meats should always be set first on the Table; and there should never be two Dishes at a Dinner of the same Sort of Meat, tho' they are diversified by boiling one and roasting the other, or baking it; but make as much Variation as you can.
> All boil'd Meats should be served first, baked Meats next, and roasted last.
> ...Boil'd Puddings of all Sorts, are for the first Course; but minc'd Pies, Tansies, Marrow Puddings, Orange Cakes, Lemon ditto, Almond ditto, and all other baked sweet Things, are for the second Course.
> Pancakes ought always to come with the first Course, and Fritters.[18]

---

available, The Modern Method of Regulating and Forming a Table...by several eminent Cooks... (London, 1750).

18. Sarah Harrison, The House-keeper's Pocket-book ... (6th edn., London, 1755), pp. 88, 107.

Yet she herself did not follow her rules rigidly. Roasted meats and fowls were often suggested for the first course, and mince pies, too, during the Christmas season, while fritters sometimes appeared in the second course. An appetizer served "before Dinner comes on the Table"--raw oysters "laid in their Shells in a Dish," for example, or thin slices of a pickled "collar" of meat--violated the two-course plan, and a selection of fruits and nuts, listed separately, was served as a third course.

The basic plan of the menu varied, of course, according to the number of guests and the size of the table, but the number of dishes in each course had to be the same. A rule of thumb might be stated thus: For a dozen diners, nine dishes in each course offered adequate variety; for eighteen people, fifteen dishes.[19] To please the eye as well as the palate, a balanced arrangement of dishes was of first importance. Featured dishes occupied the top, bottom and central positions on the table; typically they were a large joint, a turkey, a pig or hare. For elegant service the platters holding top and bottom dishes were a matching pair. Side dishes, too, were served in matching

---

19. Again Mrs. Harrison offers exceptions to the rule with family dinners of five, four, or three dishes in each course. Ibid., pp. 108-123. Yet these dinners are not so simple as they appear in diagram because the accompanying vegetables, garnishes, and sauces her menus require with each meat dish are not shown separately.

pairs of bowls or platters so that the whole arrangement was an elaborate scheme of balanced pairs: end-to-end, side-to-side, and cross-corners. The only odd dish occupied the spot in the center, where modern hostesses place elaborate flower arrangements; for the first course it might have been a haunch of venison, a huge meat pie or a mock turtle, and for the second a pyramid of jellies, tarts or sweetmeats.

Contemporary table diagrams were limited to the arrangement of the articles of food; presumably individual place settings and the accessories needed for serving the food were added by the hostess at her own discretion. If her table service followed the French fashion, which was in general use in Virginia by mid-century, she would carve and serve the top dish while the host served the bottom dish. Each of the other dishes would be served by the person seated nearest it, with diners passing their plates about the table to be served as they wished.[20] A table set for French service, therefore, required accompanying sauces and relishes to be placed beside each dish along with serving implements. Guests' plates, glasses, knives,

---

20. The older English service had required the hostess to carve and serve every dish for every guest. Modern service "from the side" by waiters who carry the dishes around the table to each guest was introduced after the middle of the nineteenth century, when it was known as service à la russe.

forks and spoons were arranged along the sides of the table somewhat in the modern manner. The exceptions were soup bowls and teacups, which were placed in front of the hostess.

Such was the fashion, which each hostess followed as nearly as she wished or was able. Guests in the homes of the Virginia gentry usually recorded favorable impressions of the quality and variety of dishes on their tables, and while no one of them ever listed a complete menu, a relatively precise composite list of popular dishes can be drawn from their comments.[21] A Virginia ham was the standing top dish, balanced by a hot meat dish of comparable size--a cut of beef or venison, a leg of lamb or

---

21. Lewis Beebe, Journal, 1776-1801, II, February 28, March 19, 1800, Historical Society of Pennsylvania, CW M-65; Andrew Burnaby, Travels through the Middle Settlements in North-America, in the Years 1759 and 1760 (London, 1775), p. 43; Francois-Jean, Marquis de Chastellux, Travels in North-America, in the Years 1780, 1781, and 1782, ed. by Howard C. Rice, Jr. (2 vols., Chapel Hill, 1963), pp. 109-110, 130-135, 386, 506; William Eddis, Letters from America... (London, 1792), pp. 22-23; William Hugh Grove, Travels in Great Britain and the Netherlands and in America, 1698-1732, University of Virginia Library; Edward M. Riley, ed., The Journal of John Harrower...1773-1776 (Williamsburg, 1963), pp. 56, 73; Robert Hunter, Quebec to Carolina in 1785-1786..., ed. by Louis B. Wright and Marion Tinling (San Marino, 1943), pp. 206-209; Benjamin H. Latrobe, The Journal of Latrobe...from 1796 to 1820 (New York, 1905), pp. 28-29; John F. D. Smyth, A Tour in the United States of America... (2 vols., London, 1784), I, 41-43, 104; Harry Toulmin, The Western Country in 1793... (San Marino, 1948), pp. 18-28, 34-43. See also Benson J. Lossing, Mount Vernon and Its Associations (New York, 1859), pp. 259, 283-284.

veal, a turkey or goose or shoat. Domestic fowls--chick-
ens, ducks, geese--supplied other meat dishes throughout
the year. Game birds, fish and seafood were popular and
plentiful in season. Since the colonists did not share
the Englishman's traditional contempt for vegetables,
guests were often surprised and pleased with the number
of them customarily served in the first course. The local
favorite,"tasty and delicious," was a leafy vegetable (cabbage or a "salad" plant) cooked with pork or beef. The
modern green salad was popular here, too, and in summer
there was a crayfish salad of salad herbs and onions mixed
with pieces of the cold seafood and dressed with vinegar
and olive oil.

The second course in Virginia was a true dessert
course, limited to sweet dishes. Apparently the colonial
housewife made no effort to duplicate the symmetrical
pattern of the first course by serving the same number of
dishes in the second, but rather arranged her dessert
table attractively and lavishly, in keeping with her tastes
and supplies. The fresh fruits available at the time were
supplemented with puddings, pies, jellies, cakes, cookies,
sweetmeats, and preserves as needed to fill out the table
design. In some households on formal occasions fruits and
nuts were served separately on a bare table as a sort of
postscript to the dinner; at this time the drinking of a

round of toasts was customary. Beverages were served with each course. In the absence of a set convention directing suitable combinations of food and drink, hosts offered a variety of wines, beer, milk, coffee and tea from which each guest made his own choice.

Little planning was needed for the family supper, which was served shortly before bedtime. It was a light meal of bread and butter, a dish of seafood or a cold meat and a sweet dish, preferably of fruit. The elaborate ball supper served at midnight was an entirely different affair, as extravagant a dessert course as could be provided. At the victory ball celebrating the Battle of Culloden, for example, Governor William Gooch served "a very handsome Collation spread on three Tables, in three different rooms, consisting of near 100 Dishes, after the most delicate Taste."[22]

Breakfast, at eight or nine o'clock, featured a variety of hot breads and cold sliced meat (Virginia ham and yesterday's roast, typically) or a hashed dish. As at dinner, there was a choice of beverage--either milk, coffee, chocolate, or tea. The menu sometimes included fruit or eggs, but these were rarities.

Tea as a meal between dinner and supper was by no

22. Virginia Gazette, July 18, 1746, p. 4.

means universal even among ladies of the upper class.

When afternoon tea was served, the beverage was accompanied by bread and butter, hot buns or crumpets or muffins, and cake.

The intelligent planning, the careful supervision, and the effort these meals demanded were usually appreciated but not always rewarded with gracious compliments. No doubt many a hostess experienced the frustrations described by Col. Landon Carter:

> I never knew the like of my family for
> finding fault. At the same time they will
> not mend things when they might if they could.
> Every[one] speak well of my table but they
> who constantly live at it. If the meat is
> very fine, it is not done says one, altho Per-
> haps nobody eat hartier of it.... If the
> Sallad is fine, the melted butter it is mixed
> up with is rank altho every mouthfull of sal-
> lad is devoured. ...and so the good folk go
> on disparaging and devouring.[23]

---

23. Diary, November 25, 1770, in Sabine Hall Papers, University of Virginia Library, CW M-1099.

kitchen of the Governor's Palace

II. THE VIRGINIA KITCHEN

In colonial Virginia, basement kitchens were more
common in the seventeenth century than in the eighteenth. As
the colonists grew more prosperous, dwelling houses grew more
comfortable, and the kitchen often became a separate building
back of the main house so that the family might be pleas-
antly removed from the heat and odors of cooking.[1] It
was a one-room structure usually, though it might have
a loft above which was used as a dry storage place or as
a bedroom for kitchen servants. For access to the loft

---

1. Robert Beverley, The History and Present State of
Virginia, ed. by Louis B. Wright (Chapel Hill, 1947), p. 290.
For an explanation of the Virginia adaptation of English arch-
itectural custom see Marcus Whiffin, The Eighteenth-Century
Houses of Williamsburg (Williamsburg, 1960), pp. 46-47.

there was a steep ladder built against the wall below the opening in the ceiling.

The kitchen was usually a bit larger than any single inside room, except for ballrooms in large plantation houses. A floor plan twelve feet square was suitable for a small kitchen; an average size was about twenty-four feet by sixteen.[2] Either brick or weatherboard might be chosen for the kitchen, often to match the dwelling house but not necessarily; there are many examples of brick kitchens with weatherboard houses and weatherboard kitchens with brick houses.

In the tidewater climate, where ventilation is especially important in summer, kitchen ceilings were higher than in other parts of the country and windows were taller. For cross-ventilation there were windows in each wall except on the chimney side, where the fireplace occupied all the wall space. The door was usually set into the wall nearest the main house and often had a window beside it.

The most satisfactory flooring was brick because it was fireproof and easy to clean. Plank flooring, equally neat and convenient, was a fire hazard. Many

---

2. See advertisements of houses and plantations for sale in the Virginia Gazettes, passim.

householders were satisfied with a well-packed dirt floor,
fireproof but hard to keep clean. Walls and ceiling were
sometimes plastered, or the walls might be finished with
sheathing; in other kitchens beams and studs showed as
open framework. Whatever the finish, walls and ceiling
were customarily whitewashed about every six months, with
successive layers of whitewash covering everything--plaster,
sheathing, open framework, and even brick nogging between
the studs.[3]

Kitchen furniture included cupboards and shelves,
chests, tables and chairs. With kitchen closets[4] all but
unknown, cupboards were especially important. There were
dressers with open graduated shelves above, double doors
below, and drawers in the middle; the housewife displayed
pewter and crockery on the shelves and stored supplies
and utensils in the drawers and behind doors which could
be locked. Other cupboards had double doors above and
below with shelves behind them. The "safes" of colonial

---

3. For many examples of whitewashing local kitchens
see Humphrey Harwood Account Book, 1776-1794, Colonial
Williamsburg Archives.

4. Pantries were equally rare. In England at the
opening of the eighteenth century the meaning of "pantry"
was changing from the original "bread room" to a cupboard
where bread and cold meat were kept; by the end of the
century it was becoming a storage place for table linen
and plate--the butler's pantry.

inventories were cupboards of this general type, though sometimes doors were of "brass wire."

Further storage facilities were provided by chests pushed against convenient wall spaces and by containers like flour barrels, traditionally covered with large flat boards, which could be used as work tables. On most plantations there were other outbuildings in the kitchen area designed for storage--notably the smoke house.

There were kitchen work tables of various sorts and sizes. The largest one, in the middle of the room, served also as a dining table for house servants in large households or for the family supper in smaller houses.

To supplement cupboard space, open shelves were placed haphazardly along the walls as needed, one at a time or in hanging sets. (The mantel shelf, a relatively common feature of Virginia taverns, was not often found in the kitchens of dwelling houses.) Working tools and the smaller utensils with handles usually hung from wall pegs of wood or iron, installed like the shelves, haphazardly.

The dominant feature of the kitchen was the big brick fireplace. The usual protection for its back wall was a layer of plaster half-an-inch thick, which was efficient and easy to replace. Though cast-iron firebacks were available in a number of sizes and designs, they were not commonly used in kitchen fireplaces because plastering was cheaper.

The indispensable piece of built-in fireplace equipment was the chimney bar or lug pole, which extended across the chimney several feet above the hearth, high up out of sight. Its function was to support the pothangers from which cooking utensils were suspended over the fire. It was usually made of iron, and its ends were set into the masonry. If made of wood, it had to be replaced fairly often. For this purpose, when the chimney was built a brick was left out of the masonry on each side to provide convenient holes into which the ends of the bar could be driven. After the bar was in place, the holes were closed, then reopened when a new bar was needed.

In well-to-do households, with large hearth space, a more elaborate support was customary--a movable crane attached to one wall of the chimney so that it would swing backward and forward like a gate and thus give the cook the advantage of hanging her pots over different parts of the hearth. In some of the great houses in the colony, as in England, two cranes might be found, one on each side of the fireplace, to supply even greater convenience for cooking a number of dishes at once.

Another desirable cooking facility, a built-in brick oven for baking bread and cakes, apparently came late to Virginia kitchens; certainly most of the sur-

viving ones date from the eighteenth century.[5] Yet, by

the decade of the 1770's they were relatively common on

the larger plantations and in the better houses and

taverns of Williamsburg.[6] Earlier ovens, of the same basic

design, were outdoor affairs, built beside chimneys, some-

times with a plastered dome or a sand covering to retain

oven under construction

---

5. For examples see the kitchens at Tuckahoe, West-
over, Stratford, and the Episcopal Rectory at Accomac
Court House. In Williamsburg reconstructed ones may be
examined at the Palace, Wythe House, Raleigh Tavern, and
Brush-Everard House.

6. Repairs are recorded in Harwood's ledgers for
William Hunter, Alexander Purdie, Benjamin Waller, Jane
Vobe, John Carter, and others.

the heat.[7] None of these baking ovens had flues,[8] and all

of them, whether inside the kitchen or outside, followed

the conventional design recommended by Mrs. Glasse:

> In the building of your oven for baking, ob-
> serve that you make it round, low roofed, and a
> little mouth; then it will take less fire, and
> keep in the heat better than a long oven and high
> roofed, and will bake the bread better.[9]

An inside oven was usually built into the cheeks of

the fireplace with its wrought-iron door set into the

face of the fireplace so that smoke from the oven fire

would escape through the chimney. Sometimes warming ovens

were built in the kitchen wall beside the fireplace, with

a separate flue leading from the top of the oven into the

chimney or chimney flue; but baking ovens were not often

---

7. A reconstructed example may be seen at the Elizabeth Reynolds house in Williamsburg; a 300-year-old example, restored, is on display at Jamestown. Before the
turn of the century the College of William and Mary had
used both kinds. The first ones "were made within the
Kitchen but when they were heated the smoke was so offen-
sive that it was found necessary to pull them down and
build others out of doors." Memorandum of Several faults
in the Building of Wm. and Mary College, c. 1704, from
the papers of the Society for the Propagation of the Gos-
pel in Foreign Parts, printed in William and Mary Quar-
terly, 2nd ser., X (1930), 70.

8. For the manner of using the oven see below pp.104-105.

9. [Hannah Glasse], The Art of Cookery...(7th edn.,
London, 1760), p. 300. For diagrams of a commercial baker's oven see Denis Diderot and others, ed., Encyclopédie,
ou Dictionnaire Raisonné de Sciences, des Arts et des Mét-
iers (35 vols., Paris, 1751-1765), Planches, II, Boulanger.

set in this location because they required an added fea-

ture to draw the smoke from the room--a hood, placed

above and in front of the oven door and leading into an

opening in the wall or ceiling.

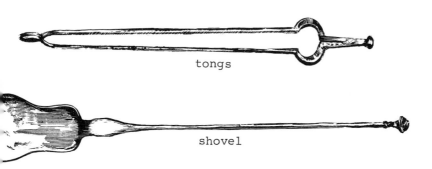

tongs

shovel

Many kinds of movable fireplace equipment were a-

vailable. To control the fire there were long-handled

iron tongs, fire forks and shovels. Tongs were either

hinged or made like sugar tongs with a spring handle.

Two-pronged fire forks, used to manipulate the larger

logs, sometimes had an additional spike at the side for

better control. Shovels were used to move hot embers

about on the hearth as needed in all the little indi-

vidual fires heating different pots.[10]

---

10. The poker came in with coal-burning grates,
which were first used in Virginia bedrooms. While wood
was so plentiful here, custom did not require metal cur-
fews to cover kitchen fires at night so as to save fuel
or kitchen bellows to blow precious embers to life in
the morning.

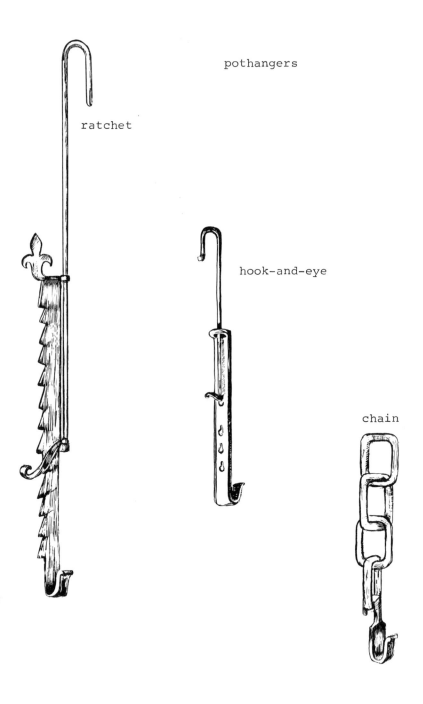

pothangers

ratchet

hook-and-eye

chain

To raise or lower the hanging pots and kettles there were iron pothangers (pothooks, trammels, or pot racks)[11] either rod-shaped or strap-shaped, with a hook at each end--one to go over the horizontal arm of the chimney crane or chimney bar, the other to hold the handle of the pot.

Pothangers were made adjustable in a number of ways. The most efficient device was a ratchet attachment, a flat bar with saw teeth on one side to catch the hook at the lower end of the pothook proper; the end of the ratchet was fitted with the flat hook from which the pot hung. A simpler arrangement applied the hook-and-eye principle. Here, the flat hanger was pierced with a series of holes down its length; the separate pothook had a small hook or knob at its upper end which could be fitted into any one of the holes, and again the holder for the handle of the pot was at the lower end of the attached rod or bar. Yet cruder devices were in common use. The chain hanger (or "jumping rope"

---

11. Appraisers used the terms interchangeably, and distinctions are no longer clear--if they ever were. Trammels seem to have been used with separate hooks, and "pothanger" or "pot rack" designated the whole fixture. A "pair of pot racks" or a "pair of pothooks" was apparently the appraiser's way of indicating an adjustable pothanger of two parts; however, there existed a simple arrangement of two hooks on a ring, which would accommodate two pots over the same small bed of coals.

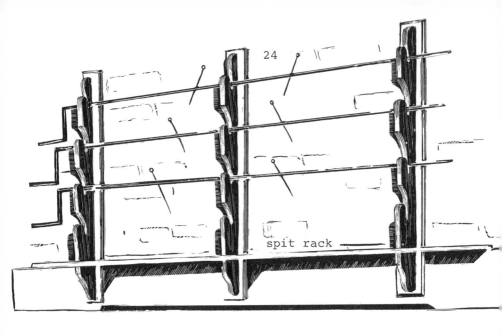

spit rack

24

still seen in old Scottish cottages) was a chain of rings
large enough to loop over the simple hook on the crane;
it could be adjusted up or down as desired.

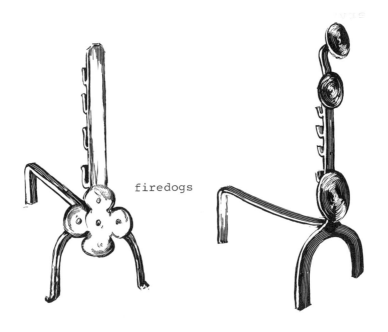

firedogs

Firedogs were needed to hold the logs of wood on the
hearth. In their simplest form the upright piece was low

enough not to interfere with the swinging pots. More desirable was a pair of andirons or spitdogs with tall front uprights fitted with a series of hooks for holding roasting spits. The iron spits came in different lengths and weights for different sizes of joints and birds. When not in use the spits were kept in a rack customarily placed on the wall above the fireplace.

For even roasting, spits had to be turned, and so they were equipped at one end with a handle, which the cook turned. To save the cook from the heat--and the meat from an inattentive cook--there were mechanical jacks of several kinds. The most efficient was a weight or clock jack, attached to the wall beside or above the fireplace; its driving wheels were connected by a chain, a leather belt, or a rope to a disk on the end of the spit opposite the handle. A smoke jack, inside the chimney, was a revolving paddle arrangement (like a child's toy windmill) turned by the up-draught of hot air; it, too, had driving wheels which could be belted to the disk on the spit. A third kind of jack was the dangle spit rotated by a winding and unwinding cord; this crude device was replaced later by the spring-driven bottle jack.

Another desirable feature of the spit was an attachment to hold the roasting meat in place as it turned. Two fork-like prongs welded to the spit in the middle would

jacks

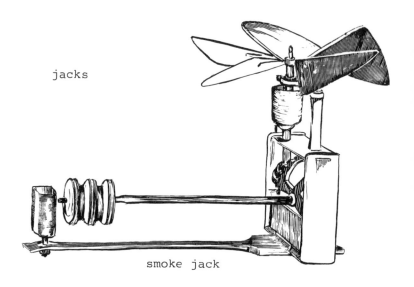

smoke jack

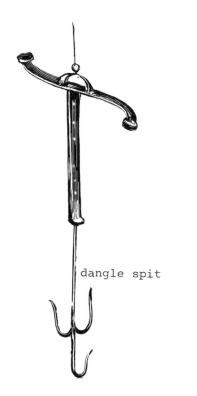

dangle spit

clock jack

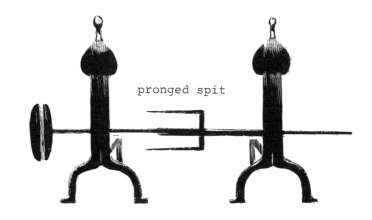

pronged spit

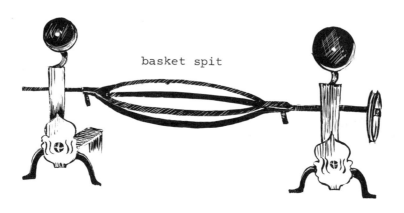

basket spit

hold a large joint steady. Small fowls or birds could be

held in place with individual skewers thrust into holes

placed at intervals along the length of the spit. A

basket or cradle spit, made of thin iron bars curved out-

ward in the center to form a cage, held a suckling pig

or a large fowl without piercing it and thus preserved

its juices.

dripping pan with basting spoon

Below each joint roasting on a spit stood a dripping pan of iron, copper or tin to collect the juices.
A long-handled basting spoon completed the necessary
roasting equipment.

For broiling there were gridirons made of parallel
iron bars in rectangular or circular frames, standing on
short legs so that the glowing embers would sear the meat
quickly. For grilling thicker slices of meat more slowly,
the gridiron was placed on a brandreth--an iron trivet or
tripod with longer legs. If the cook wished to brown the
top of a dish (as her modern counterpart uses the top grill
of her electric oven), she held a red-hot salamander over
it, moving it about to produce the desired color.

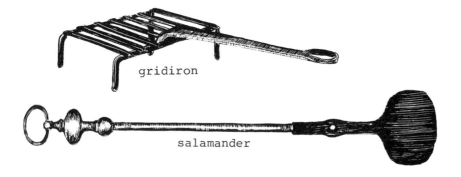

gridiron

salamander

tin Dutch oven

For roasting birds there was a tin or copper Dutch oven shaped like half a cylinder, with a spit set in the axis. When in use the open side of the roaster faced the fire so that the bird was quickly cooked by direct heat and by radiation from the rounded side. A little door in the curved surface enabled the cook to test the bird without moving the oven away from the fire.

frying pan on trivet

frying pan with legs

Frying pans were long-handled and shallow, made of thin sheets of iron, copper or brass. Those that stood on their own three legs (called spiders in nineteenth-century America) could be placed directly over hot coals; those without legs had to be held over the fire or set on trivets.

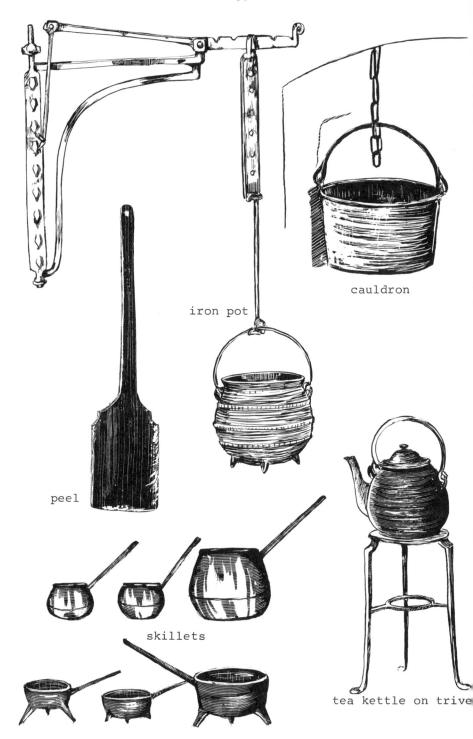

cauldron

iron pot

peel

skillets

tea kettle on trive

Since more articles of food were boiled or stewed than were roasted or fried, the most common utensils were for boiling. Large pots, kettles, and cauldrons made of iron, copper, or brass were equipped with bails (arched, bucket-like handles) so that they could be suspended from pothangers, and some of them had their own fitted lids. Only the iron pots had short feet as well as bails. Smaller, footed stewing pots called skillets had long rigid handles like those of frying pans and were about as deep as they were wide. Skillets came in brass, copper, or bell metal, sometimes with iron feet and handles. Stew-pans and saucepans were members of the skillet family, usually footed, though sometimes made with flat bottoms.

There were special kinds of kettles: tea kettles, with or without feet, the larger ones made of iron; preserving kettles, wide and shallow, preferably of tin or tinned copper; fish kettles, also of tin or copper, oval and shallow, with fitted lids and inside fish "plates" or draining racks.

For oven baking a wooden peel was needed to place the baking load in the hot oven. Tin baking pans were available for bread, cakes, pies, tarts and biscuits (i.e., cookies). Cake pans were often described as garths or hoops, shapes or molds, suitable for pound cakes--not layer cakes--and these molds also came in

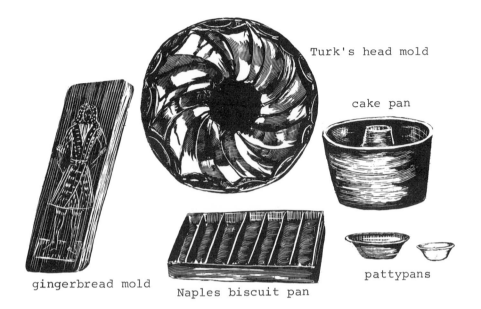

Turk's head mold

cake pan

gingerbread mold

Naples biscuit pan

pattypans

earthenware. Pattypans for baking tarts or pasties were
usually plain, small pie pans but they also came in fancy
shapes, like molds. The most popular special biscuit tin
was the Naples pan, characterized by parallel partitions; other biscuits were baked on tin sheets or in pie
pans. Gingerbread molds were usually made of wood, often
in elaborate designs.

For fireplace baking there was an iron Dutch oven
or bake kettle, footed like the standard iron pot but not
so tall and with a flat, tight-fitting lid. Iron griddles
(girdles or baking irons) for scones, muffins, buns, oatcakes, corn pone and the like were flat circles fitted
with bails. A Virginia substitute for the primitive baking stone was the bread hoe or hoecake baker--a farmer's

iron Dutch oven

hoe

griddle

broad hoe brought into the kitchen.

Though they were rare, wafer irons and waffle irons were in use in the colony. The wafer iron, originally used for sacramental wafers, also baked thin, crisp dessert wafers in elaborate designs. The larger waffle iron of simpler grid design came into fashion at the end of the colonial period, to bake the sweet bread we still call a waffle.

There were toasters of several kinds: the long-handled fork with two or three tines; footed bread toasters that would accommodate several slices at a time, most of them equipped with a simple revolving mechanism; cheese toasters, which looked like small tin Dutch ovens fitted with shelves in place of spits.

In other places in her kitchen--cupboards, shelves, pegs, chests, drawers, tables--the Virginia housewife kept other utensils and tools. As one would expect, many

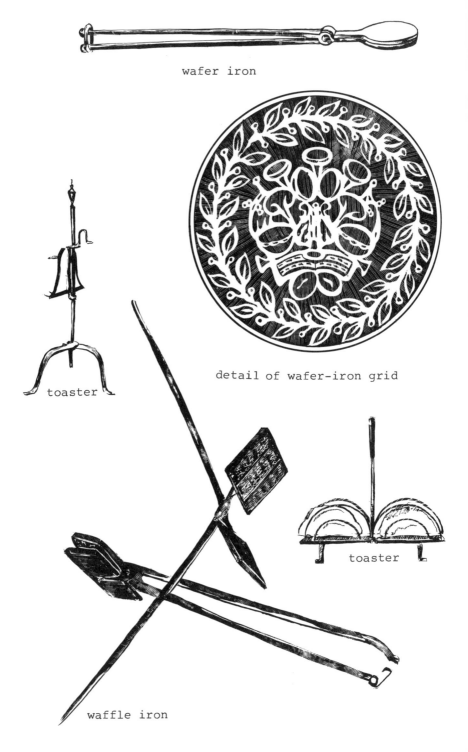

wafer iron

detail of wafer-iron grid

toaster

toaster

waffle iron

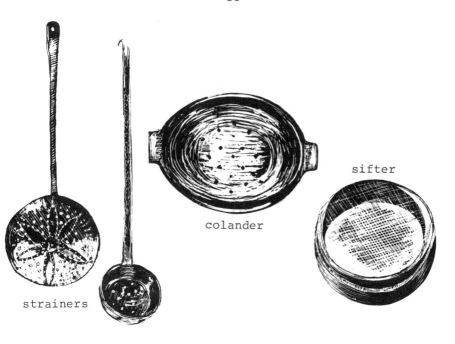

sifter

colander

strainers

were made of wood: bread troughs, rolling pins, pastry

boards and cutting boards, spoons, bowls, and trenchers.

Kitchen bowls and basins, plates and platters also came

in stoneware, earthenware and pewter. Colanders similar

to modern ones were made of tin, pewter, brass, or pottery.

Sieves had hair-screen or wire-screen bottoms and round

sides of metal or wood. Sifters and searces, also round,

were usually wooden-bodied with mesh bottoms of silk, lawn,

or hair. Strainers, on the other hand, resembled long-

handled spoons or shallow ladles, their large brass bowls

pierced with holes arranged in designs that were often

quite decorative.

Short-handled mixing spoons, similar to modern table-

spoons, were made of pewter or wood. Long-handled ladles

and stirring spoons, for use in cooking pots, were often
made of iron, sometimes of brass or copper. Kitchen knives,
generally with wooden handles, came in several sizes and
shapes; there were chopping knives, butcher knives, carving knives, paring knives and meat cleavers. Kitchen
forks had three tines usually, though the flesh fork used
with roasting meats might have only two prongs.

Metal graters, semi-cylindrical in shape, varied in
size according to the fineness of the grated material to
be produced; coarse bread graters, for example, and fine
nutmeg graters can be distinguished in inventory lists.
There were mills for grinding coffee, with wooden cases
and iron grinding parts. Smaller pepper mills existed,
but they were not often found in Virginia. Most grinding

slicer

mortar and pestle

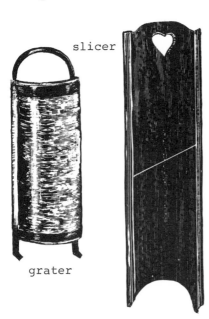

grater

coffee mill

chores were performed with mortar and pestle. Small spice

mortars and pestles were made of brass, bell metal, or

marble. Larger mortars of wood or iron were used with

iron pestles; this combination for making home-ground corn

meal was one of the two basic requirements for Virginia

households, the other being the iron cooking pot.

There were containers of many sizes, shapes and ma-

terials. Wooden tubs could be used for washing chores of

all kinds and for salting meat. Wooden barrels, casks,

kegs and rundlets held large quantities of liquid or dry

supplies, though they were not necessarily stored in the

kitchen. Smaller containers included buckets and pails

of wood or brass, wooden piggins, butter firkins, and

churns. Baskets of woven straw or splints were available

in a variety of shapes and sizes. There also were wooden

dry measures with capacities ranging from a bushel to a

pint. Sets of liquid measures ranging from a gallon to

a gill were commonly made of pewter and shaped like mugs

or steins, with handles but often without lids.

Jars, jugs, and storage pots of earthenware and

stoneware were often beautifully shaped and decorated.

There were also pans--notably milk pans--made of the same

materials. Glass bottles in large numbers were standard

entries in Virginia household inventories; glass jars were

baskets

wooden dry measures

pewter liquid measures

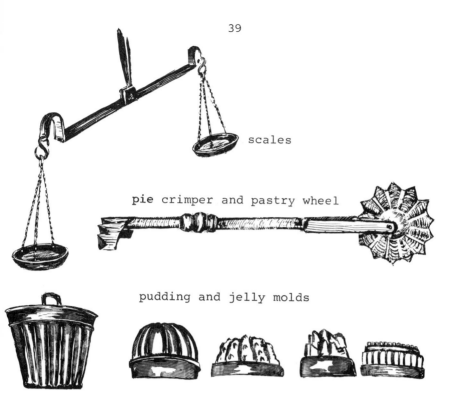

scales

pie crimper and pastry wheel

pudding and jelly molds

very rare or else appraisers included them among the bottles.

Since there were no standardized measuring cups and spoons, cookbooks often specified the amount of an ingredient by weight. For this reason a set of scales and weights was an important piece of kitchen equipment.

Though the labor-saving devices and gadgets that characterize today's American kitchens were unthought of in colonial times, in some of the great houses there were luxury items in kitchen equipment which were used to add a note of elegance to the food and the service. Jelly molds in a variety of elaborate shapes were available in tin and copper. Pies, tarts, and pasties were decorated with pie crimpers and pastry wheels (Mrs. Bradley's jaggs

and runners). With shredders, slicers, sugar nippers,
lemon squeezers, and coffee roasters, the cook could ease
her labors and improve the appearance and texture of the
food.

Plate warmers and hot-water plates offered partial
solutions to the problem of getting the food still hot
from the kitchen to the dining room. Finally, at the end
of the period there were chafing dishes of silver or copper
which could be placed on the dining table; earlier chafing
dishes or "stoves" were kitchen utensils of iron or earthenware with built-in fire pans.

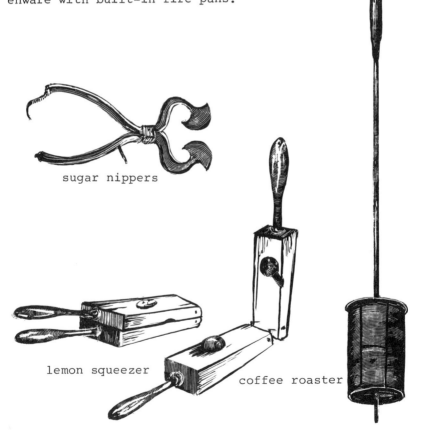

sugar nippers

lemon squeezer

coffee roaster

III. COOKING METHODS: BOILING AND STEWING

With an iron pot the basic cooking equipment, the
poor presumably boiled or stewed all their meat and vegetables, while the well-to-do found the procedure the
simplest and stewed dishes often the tastiest. Mrs.
Bradley defined the process:

> Boiling is the Dressing Things by Means
> of Water, as Roasting does it by the naked
> Fire; this is the whole Difference, but in
> general Boiling is the easiest Way, as it
> requires less Nicety and Attendance. To
> keep the Water really boiling all the Time,
> to have the Meat clean, and to know how long
> is required for doing the Joint, or other
> Thing boiled, comprehends almost the whole
> Art and Mystery.[1]

The authorities[2] agreed that a large cut of meat--
a leg, loin, breast, neck, rump or haunch--should be put
into cold salted water and placed over a large clear fire

---

1. Martha Bradley, The British Housewife... (London, [c. 1770]), p. 37.

2. Ibid., pp. 37-39; [Hannah Glasse], The Art of
Cookery... (7th edn., London, 1760), pp. 8-9; Sarah Harrison, The House-keeper's Pocket-book... (6th edn., London, 1755), pp. 19-21; Elizabeth Raffald, The Experienced
English House-keeper... (4th edn., London, 1775), pp. 52-
53; Mary Randolph, The Virginia Housewife... (Philadelphia,
1855), p. 27. E. Smith, The Compleat Housewife... (Williamsburg, 1742) gives no general boiling rules but agrees
on principles in individual recipes.

for steady, even cooking. The general rule for cooking time was fifteen minutes per pound, beginning the count when the pot came to a boil. The immediate and careful removal of the scum as it collected on top of the water engaged the cook's full attention in the early stages of cooking; then, after the liquid cleared, she covered the pot and let it simmer untended while she regulated the fire.

In the colony the most popular standing dish was a boiled joint, the famous Virginia-cured ham. As there are many "traditional" ways of curing it, so with the cooking. All recipes agree that it must be soaked for some time--overnight, twenty-four hours, or thirty-six-- and then simmered slowly in "plenty of water." Individual cooks add to the water whatever flavoring agents they please--cider, wine, beer, spices, or nothing at all --and they know it is done when "the bone on the under part comes off with ease." In Mrs. Randolph's day it was already customary to give it further attention after boiling it. She skinned it, then covered the top with bread crumbs and put it in an oven to brown.[3]

---

3. Randolph, Virginia Housewife, pp. 50, 54; for curing directions see below pp. 183-184. A collection of nineteenth-century recipes may be found in Marion Cabell Tyree, Housekeeping in Old Virginia (Louisville, 1879; reprint edn. 1965).

Contemporary tastes in England and in Virginia required that joints of veal and house-lamb come out of the pot white and plump. Mrs. Glasse, Mrs. Bradley and Mrs. Raffald relied on cleanliness, slow cooking, and careful skimming to produce the desired effect. Mrs. Raffald warned against the use of milk or oatmeal "to make it white" but with Mrs. Harrison and Mrs. Randolph approved a light dusting with fine flour as part of the preparation of the meat.

There was some disagreement about the advisability of wrapping a joint in a floured cloth before boiling it. In general this extra care for preserving the shape was reserved for articles that were stuffed with forcemeat, because a cloth sometimes affected color and flavor adversely.

To "force" a joint one removed a large part of the meat from inside the cut, chopped it or ground it with a pestle, and combined it with egg yolk, suet, bread crumbs, herbs, spices, and other seasonings to form a stuffing. Mrs. Custis copied out a number of recipes for such dishes suitable for elegant company, among them:

> To boyle a Legg of muton the forc'd way.
>
> Take a large legg of muton, & take forth the leane & mince it very small, with a pound of suet & put to it a handfull of sweet hearbs shread small, halfe a pound of currans & halfe a pound of sugar, 6 egg youlks, mace, cloves,

& nutmegg beaten, a good handfull of grated
bread, & a little salt, worke all these together with your hand, & put halfe of it into
the scinn of your legg of muton, & make 20 or
30 little balls of what you leave out, & role
the rest in 2 rouls role them in grated bread,
& after in youlks of eggs & bake them, & wrap
the legg in a cloth & boyle it. take 10 or 12
of the balls, & when the legg is allmoste boyled, take allmoste a quart of the broth &
streyne it into a deepe dish, & poure the
liquor into it out of your bakt forct meate, &
take the rest of your balls & put them into
this broth, set them on a chafing dish of char-
cole, & make it boyle, & put in 3 or 4 hard
eggs shread, 4 youlks of eggs beaten with 4
spoonfulls of vinegar, put in some parsley
shread small, & stir all these together, & put
in a little sugar, then lay your legg in a
large dish, & poure the sauce all over it, lay
in sippets. and cut the bakd balls in halves,
and lay them about the dish, with tostes fry'd
in eggs, and parsley fryed and hard youlks of
eggs and barberyes. & soe serve it up. the
youlks of eggs you lay about your dish must
allsoe be cut in halves.[4]

Long strips and flat cuts of meat were often "col-

lared," i.e., rolled into tight cylinders and firmly tied

in place. Here the shape was important because a cold

collar, sliced, was an attractive supper dish. A typical

example is Mrs. Smith's:

To Collar a Breast of Veal.

Take a Breast of Veal and bone it, and
wash it, and dry it in a clean Cloth; then
shred Thyme, Winter-savoury, and Parsley, very
small, and mix it with Salt, Pepper, Cloves,
Mace, and Nutmeg; then strew it on the In-side
of your Meat, and roll it up hard, beginning
at the Neck End; tie it up with Tape, and put

---

4. Frances Parke Custis, A Booke of Cookery, No. 200.

it in a Pot fit to boil it in, standing upright: You must boil it in Water and Salt,
and a bunch of Sweet-herbs; when 'tis boiled
enough, take it off the Fire, and put it in an
earthen Pot, and when the Liquor is cold pour
it over it, or else boil Salt and Water strong
enough to bear an Egg; and when that is cold,
pour it on your Veal: When you serve it to
the Table, cut it in round Slices. Garnish
with Laurel or Fennel.[5]

Fowls of all kinds, domestic and wild, were often

boiled "in a good deal" of salted water, preferably with-

out a cloth. Mrs. Glasse offered a practical rule of

thumb for cooking time: "A little chicken will be done in

fifteen minutes, a large chicken in twenty minutes, a good

fowl in half an hour, a little turky or goose in an hour,

and a large turky in an hour and a half."[6] While a fowl

prepared so simply could be delicious served with a simple

sauce, it did not answer the requirements of interesting

appearance and cookbooks provided elaborate instructions

for dressing it up for company. Two recipes from Mrs.

Custis's collection illustrate popular refinements:

> A Capon after the Flanders fashion.
>
> Boyle your Capon in a quart of white wine
> another of water & the rest of muton broth, cut

---

5. Smith, Compleat Housewife, pp. 18-19. For other
cuts see Ibid., 12, 17, 24; Glasse, Art of Cookery, pp. 30-
31, 254-255; Harrison, Pocket-book, pp. 136-139; Raffald,
English House-keeper, pp. 273, 300-304. For similar treatment of smaller slices of meat see "olives" in made dishes,
pp. 160-161.

6. Glasse, Art of Cookery, p. 9.

in some carrots & put in 2 marrow bones, whole
mace & some sugar serve it up in some of the
broth with sops, but leave out the marrow bones.[7]

To boyle Pigeons with Puddings.

When your Pigeons are clean drest boyle
them in water & salt, then bake for the pudding some grated bread a little flower, 3 or
4 eggs, & a little creame. take marrow or
beefe suet shread small, mace nutmegg & cinnamon to your taste, & a little sack, for
hearbs take a little sweete margerum tarragon
& sorrell. mix all these together pritty
stiff adding a few currans. then take cloaths
wet them & flower them & tie the pudding meat
in severall partitions about the biggness of
an egge, & boyle them with your pigeons, when
they are boyled make this sauce. a little
white wine & butter, a little verges & sugar,
then put in 2 youlks of eggs well beaten, when
you dish them up, set a sprigg of roasmary in
the breast of each pigeon & betwixt every pigeon a pudding, poure on the sauce & soe serve
them up.[8]

The procedure for preparing stewed dishes was similar.

Though the distinction between boiling and stewing was not

always precise, in general large pieces of meat or whole

fowls were boiled in a great deal of water, in an iron pot

or large brass kettle suspended from a pothanger or stand-

ing over a bed of coals; the liquid would be discarded or

put aside for later use as broth. A stewed dish was sim-

mered, covered, in a relatively shallow pan of iron or

copper standing over coals; less liquid was used because

---

7. Custis, Booke of Cookery, No. 38.

8. Ibid., No. 21.

all of it would be served with the meat as gravy or sauce.

The usual stew was made of relatively small pieces

of meat, sliced or chopped. Especially popular was the

dish called collops, i.e., slices. For Scotch collops

Mrs. Custis directed:

> Take a legg of muton or veale or fresh
> beefe, cut them in thin slyces, & lay them
> on a table₀ beat them with the back of your
> knife, then steep them in vinegar or verges.
> after lay them in a frying pan, put to them
> a pint of strong broth, & halfe a pinte of
> faire water, & put into it a bunch of time,
> sweete marjerum & winter savory, & an ounion,
> & let them boyle till their meat be tender,
> then pour out your liquor into a dish & put
> to it a little manchet cut like dice, an-
> chovis capers or oysters & leamon minced, &
> a piece of fresh butter, when they are boyld
> enough, take your sops & fry them in fresh
> butter till they are crisp, then lay them
> in your dish & pour on your sause, serve
> them up with sippets & garnish your dish
> with leamons & capers.[9]

Or they might be served in their own gravy, as directed

by Mrs. Glasse:

Beef collops.

> Cut them into thin pieces about two inches
> long, beat them with a back of a knife very
> well, grate some nutmeg, flour them a little,
> lay them in a stew-pan, put in as much water
> as you think will do for sauce, half an onion
> cut small, a little piece of lemon-peel cut
> small, a bundle of sweet herbs, a little pep-
> per and salt, a piece of butter rolled in a
> little flour. Set them on a slow fire: when
> they begin to simmer, stir them now and then;
> when they begin to be hot, ten minutes will

---

9. Ibid., No. 4.

do them, but take care they don't boil. Take
out the sweet herbs, pour it into the dish,
and send it to table.

Note, you may do the inside of a surloin of beef
in the same manner, the day after it is roasted,
only don't beat them, but cut them thin.[10]

Leftovers from a large roast, a boiled joint or a

fowl when sliced and stewed in this way were properly

called a hash. This is Mrs. Custis's recipe for

A hash of muton or veale.

Cut you meat very thin, & set it on the
fire. put to it a few capers & liquor, 2 or
3 ounions, a little spinnage, mint or what
other hearbs you please, put in a little vinegar water, gravie & some butter, soe let it
stew 2 houres before you serve it up.[11]

If a brown gravy was desired, the slices might be

browned quickly in butter before the liquid and season-

ings were added, or after the meat had been simmered to

tenderness, as Mrs. Glasse directed for stewed beef steaks:

Take rump steaks, pepper and salt them,
lay them in a stew-pan, pour in half a pint
of water, a blade or two of mace, two or three
cloves, a little bundle of sweet herbs, an
anchovy, a piece of butter rolled in flour, a
glass of white wine, and an onion; cover them
close, and let them stew softly till they are
tender, then take out the steaks, flour them,
fry them in fresh butter, and pour away all

---

10. Glasse, Art of Cookery, pp. 37-38; cf. Mrs.
Harrison's "White Scotch Collops," Pocket-book, p. 23,
with a cream gravy.

11. Custis, Booke of Cookery, No. 9. Claret could
be used instead of vinegar, especially in beef hash. Harrison, Pocket-book, pp. 24-25.

the fat, strain the sauce they were stewed in,
and pour into the pan; toss it all up together
till the sauce is quite hot and thick. If you
add a quarter of a pint of oysters, it will
make it the better. Lay the steaks into the
dish, and pour the sauce over them. Garnish
with any pickle you like.[12]

This was the basic procedure in preparing the fricassees

and ragouts imported from France in the late seventeenth

century.[13]

While a single stewpan was considered an adequate

cooking utensil for stewed dishes, there was a popular

combination of chafing dish and a pair of matching pewter

dishes which offered several advantages. The chafing dish

of hot embers could be placed outside the hearth or even

outside the kitchen, in another room. Moreover, its heat

was easier to control for steady simmering. The two pewter

dishes, placed together like a kettle with a close-fitting

lid, kept the steam and odor and flavor inside; and they

could be taken directly from the chafing dish to the table.

Mrs. Glasse explained their use in this recipe:

A pretty way of stewing chickens.

Take two fine chickens, half boil them,
then take them up in a pewter, or silver dish,
if you have one; cut up your fowls, and separate all the joint-bones one from another,

---

12. Glasse, Art of Cookery, p. 38.

13. For fricassees and ragouts see below, pp. 153-156.

and then take out the breast-bones. If there
is not liquor enough from the fowls add a few
spoonfuls of water they were boiled in, put
in a blade of mace, and a little salt; cover
it close with another dish, set it over a
stove or a chafing-dish of coals, let it stew
till the chickens are enough, and then send
them hot to the table in the same dish they
were stewed in.

N.B. You may do rabbits, partridges, or moor-
game this way.[14]

And Mrs. Custis in this one:

To Stew Calves Feet.

Boyle & pill them, then put them between
2 dishes over a chafing dish of coles, with
some water, & put therein a little vinegar
some currans, sugar cinnamon & mace & when
they are enough you may if you pleas put in
a piece of fresh butter & soe serve them up.[15]

A stewed dish might be made very elaborate indeed
by adding a variety of unusual or exotic ingredients to
the sauce or garnish. Beef royal, for example, was elegant enough for the most fastidious guest at dinner or
supper:

Take a surloin of beef, or a large rump,
bone it and beat it very well, then lard it
with bacon, season it all over with salt,
pepper, mace, cloves, and nutmeg, all beat
fine, some lemon-peel cut small, and some
sweet herbs; in the mean time make a strong
broth of the bones, take a piece of butter
with a little flour, brown it, put in the
beef, keep it turning often till it is brown,
then strain the broth, put all together into

14. Glasse, _Art of Cookery_, p. 76.

15. Custis, Booke of Cookery, No. 43.

a pot, put in a bay-leaf, a few truffles, and
some ox palates cut small; cover it close,
and let it stew till it is tender, take out
the beef, skim off all the fat, pour in a pint
of claret, some fried oysters, an anchovy, and
some gerkins shred small; boil all together,
put in the beef to warm, thicken your sauce
with a piece of butter rolled in flour, or
mushroom powder, or burnt butter. Lay your
meat in the dish, pour the sauce over it, and
send it to the table. This may be eat either
hot or cold.[16]

Fowls, too, might be dressed up in comparable fash-
ion--Mrs. Smith's stewed turkey, for example:

Take a fine young Turkey, kill'd, pull'd,
and drawn; fill the Skin on the Breast with
Forc'd-meat, and lard it on the Sides with
Bacon; Put into the Belly half an Eschalot,
two Anchovies, and a little Thyme shred small;
brown it in a Pan with a little Butter; when
'tis very brown, put it in a Stew-pan, with
strong Gravy, some White-wine, or Claret, two
or three Anchovies, some Mace, Sweet-herbs, a
little Pepper, and let it stew till 'tis thoroughly enough; then thicken the Liquor with
Butter and Eggs; fry some French Loaves dipp'd
in Cream, after the Top and the Crumb is taken
out; then fill them with stew'd Oysters or
Shrimps, or Cockles, and with them garnish the
Dish, or with sliced Lemon. A Hen, Goose, or
Duck, does well this way.[17]

The boiled fish associated with French cuisine in
modern America was then a great favorite in England and

---

16. Glasse, Art of Cookery, p. 42; cf. Mrs. Harrison's Leg of Mutton à la Royale, Pocket-book, p. 21.
Note that these stews contain no vegetables except pot
herbs and onions; potatoes and carrots were added to
stews in the nineteenth century.

17. Smith, Compleat Housewife, p. 29; cf. pigeons,
ducks, and wild fowl in Harrison, Pocket-book, pp. 29-30.

the colonies, and good cooks were careful about its appearance. Mrs. Glasse urged her readers to handle all sorts of flat fish gently to avoid breaking them, and to drain them well before placing them in serving dishes. "If there be any water in your dish with the boiled fish," she cautioned, "take it out with a sponge."[18] Special utensils for handling fish were relatively common in the better equipped kitchens: a long oval fish kettle of tin, brass or copper, fitted with a rack in the bottom called a "fish plate," and a "fish slice" for removing the cooked fish from the kettle without breaking it, and yet draining it adequately. Mrs. Glasse's directions for boiling turbot were applicable to any large fish that could be served whole:

> Lay it in a good deal of salt and water an hour or two, and if it is not quite sweet, shift your water five or six times; first put a good deal of salt in the mouth and belly.
> In the mean time set on your fish kettle with clean water and salt, a little vinegar, and a piece of horse-raddish. When the water boils, lay the turbutt on a fish-plate, put it into the kettle, let it be well boiled, but take great care it is not too much done; when enough, take off the fish-kettle, set it before the fire, then carefully lift up the fish-plate and set it across the kettle to drain: in the mean time melt a good deal of fresh butter, and bruise in either the body of one or two lobsters, and the meat cut small,

---

18. Glasse, <u>Art of Cookery</u>, "To dress flat fish," p. 178.

then give it a boil, and pour it into basons.
This is the best sauce; but you may make what
you please. Lay the fish in the dish. Garnish with scraped horse-raddish and lemon, and
pour a few spoonfuls of sauce over it.[19]

Or it could be stewed in white wine, as directed by Mrs.

Custis:

> To dress A Pike Carpe Tub or large trout.
>
> Take your fish & scale it & slyt it alive
> & wash it with white wine, & take the blood
> & as much white wine as will cover it, putting
> a fish plate in the bottom of your kettle, &
> some large mace with a bundle of sweet hearbs,
> as time parsley & sweet margerum, let it have
> one boyle then take it of and let it stew lea-
> surely, then bone 6 anchovis & put into the
> liquor, then take 3 quarters of a pound of good
> fresh butter, & let them stew together a little
> while, then take up your fish & shake up your
> butter anchovis & broth alltogether & poure it
> on your fish & dish it up with sippets.[20]

If the fish kettle was not equipped with a fish plate,

a cloth might be used, as suggested by Mrs. Glasse:

> To dress salmon au court-bouillon.
>
> After having washed and made your salmon
> very clean, score the side pretty deep, that
> it may take the seasoning, take a quarter of
> an ounce of mace, a quarter of an ounce of
> cloves, a nutmeg, dry them and beat them fine,
> a quarter of an ounce of black pepper beat
> fine, and an ounce of salt. Lay the salmon in
> a napkin, season it well with this spice, cut
> some lemon-peel fine, and parsley, throw all
> over, and in the notches put about a pound of
> fresh butter rolled in flour, roll it up tight

---

19. _Ibid._, p. 172.

20. Custis, Booke of Cookery, No. 191; cf. Mrs.
Smith's boiled pike, p. 17.

in the napkin, and bind it about with packthread. Put it in a fish-kettle, just big
enough to hold it, pour in a quart of white
wine, a quart of vinegar, and as much water
as will just boil it.

Set it over a quick fire, cover it close;
when it is enough, which you must judge by
the bigness of your salmon, set it over a
stove[21] to stew till you are ready. Then
have a clean napkin folded in the dish it is
to lay in, turn it out of the napkin it was
boiled in on the other napkin. Garnish the
dish with a good deal of parsley crisped before the fire.

For sauce have nothing but plain butter
in a cup, or horse-raddish and vinegar.
Serve it up for a first course.[22]

Shellfish also were commonly boiled or stewed.

Lobsters, crabs, cockles and mussels were first parboiled

in their shells and then dressed in various ways. Prawns,

shrimps, crawfish and oysters were usually shelled and

then stewed in white wine and seasonings. Buttered shell-

fish was a favorite dish:

To butter crabs or lobsters.

Take two crabs, or lobsters, being boiled,
and cold, take all the meat out of the shells
and bodies, mince it small, and put it all together into a sauce-pan; add to it a glass of
white wine, two spoonfuls of vinegar, a nutmeg
grated, then let it boil up till it is thorough
hot. Then have ready half a pound of fresh
butter, melted with an anchovy, and the yolks
of two eggs beat up and mixed with the butter;
then mix crab and butter all together, shaking
the sauce-pan constantly round till it is
quite hot. Then have ready the great shell,

---

21. A kitchen chafing dish.

22. Glasse, Art of Cookery, p. 177.

either of the crab, or lobster; lay it in the
middle of your dish, pour some into the shell,
and the rest in little saucers round the shell,
sticking three-corner toasts between the saucers, and round the shell. This is a fine
side-dish at a second course.[23]

Or:

Buttered shrimps.

Stew two quarts of shrimps in a pint of
white wine, with nutmeg, beat up eight eggs,
with a little white wine and half a pound of
butter, shaking the sauce-pan one way all the
time over the fire till they are thick enough,
lay toasted sippets round a dish, and pour
them over it, so serve them up.[24]

Mrs. Custis preferred a simpler treatment:

To butter Shrimps.

First take your shrimps after they are
boyled & set them on coles till they are verry
hot; then melt your butter & beat it very thick
& poure it on them when they are served up, &
strew on some pepper.[25]

For oysters she recommended this recipe:

To Stew Oysters.

Take your oysters open & pick them very
clean & save the liquor that comes out of them,
when you open them set on a scyllet of water,
& make it boyle but not to fast, then put in
your oysters & make them boyle up, then take
them up & put them in a cullender, & poure
cold water on them this is to plump & keepe
them from shrinking then set them a stewing
in theyr owne liquor & as much water as will

---

23. *Ibid.*, p. 185. For a sauce of sack, sugar,
mace, and lemon juice see Harrison, *Pocket-book*, p. 42.

24. *Ibid.*, p. 194.

25. Custis, Booke of Cookery, No. 183.

cover them, or put to the liquor white wine
in the roome of water, put in a whole ounion
some whole pepper, & whole mace, when you
serve them up, put in butter & garnish your
dish with beaten & sifted ginger.[26]

At mid-century the fashion for a shorter cooking
time was reflected by Mrs. Raffald:

To stew OYSTERS, and all sorts of SHELL FISH.

When you have opened your oysters, put
their liquor into a tossing pan with a little
beaten mace, thicken it with flour and butter,
boil it three or four minutes, toast a slice
of white bread, and cut it into three-cornered
pieces, lay them round your dish, put in a
spoonful of good cream, put in your oysters,
and shake them round in your pan, you must not
let them boil, for if they do it will make
them hard and look small, serve them up in a
little soup dish or plate.

N.B. You may stew cockles, muscles, or any
shell fish the same way.[27]

To stew OYSTERS, COCKLES, and MUSCLES.

Open your fish clean from the shell, save
the liquor, and let it stand to settle, then
strain it through a hair sieve, and put to it
as many crumbs of bread as will make it pretty
thick, and boil them well together before you
put in the fish, with a good lump of butter,
pepper, and salt to your taste, give them a
single boil, and serve them up.

N.B. You may make it a fish sauce by adding
a glass of white wine just before you take it
off the fire, and leaving out the crumbs of
bread.[28]

---

26. Ibid., No. 182.

27. Raffald, English House-keeper, p. 38.

28. Ibid., pp. 38-39.

Hot liquids were prepared in great variety--broths,

soups, gruels, pottages, porridges. Broths were made

from liquids in which meat, fowl or fish had been boiled

or they could be prepared from scraps and the less de-

sirable parts of animals and fowls. Nourishing and eco-

nomical, they were served at table accompanied by sippets

or toasted penny loaves, or they could be put aside for

later use in sauces, gravies and made dishes. They were

important in invalid cookery, for the cook was also the

family nurse.

Soups were basically broths, flavored with pot herbs,

onions, sometimes carrots and turnips, but served clear

with pieces of meat and toasts. Mrs. Glasse summarized:

Rules to be observed in making soops or broths.

First take great care the pots, or saucepans and covers be very clean and free from
all grease and sand, and that they be well
tinned, for fear of giving the broths and
soops any brassy taste. If you have time
to stew as softly as you can, it will both
have a finer flavour, and the meat will be
tenderer. But then observe, when you make
soops or broth for present use, if it is to
be done softly, don't put much more water
than you intend to have soop or broth; and
if you have the convenience of an earthen
pan or pipkin, and set it on wood embers
till it boils, then skim it, and put in your
seasoning; cover it close, and set it on embers, so that it may do very softly for some
time, and both the meat and broths will be
delicious. You must observe in all broths
and soops that one thing does not taste more
than another; but that the taste be equal,
and it has a fine agreeable relish, according to what you design it for; and you must

be sure, that all the greens and herbs you
put in be cleaned, washed, and picked.[29]

An example of the variety of meats that might be

used together is Mrs. Custis's French broth:

> Take a leane piece of beefe, a piece of
> veale or muton & a hen & boyle them in a pot
> & scum them, put in some large mace & halfe
> a cabbage if a little one, some sweet hearbs,
> as lettice & spinnage &c. boyle them well
> till all the goodness be out, then put in
> the bottom of a house-hould lofe, toward the
> end roste a leane piece of beefe & cut it
> often for gravie, draine your broth clear
> from the bottom & boyle some pigeons in salt
> & water & save a piece of cabbedge to put in
> the middle of your dish. Let it stand on
> coles, after the pigeons gravie & broth is in.[30]

For economy Mrs. Randolph recommended:

> SOUP OF ANY KIND OF OLD FOWL.
> The only way in which they are eatable.
>
> Put the fowls in a coop and feed them
> moderately for a fortnight; kill one and
> cleanse it, cut off the legs and wings, and
> separate the breast from the ribs, which,
> together with the whole back, must be thrown
> away, being too gross and strong for use.
> Take the skin and fat from the parts cut off
> which are also gross. Wash the pieces nicely,
> and put them on the fire with about a pound
> of bacon, a large onion chopped small, some
> pepper and salt, a few blades of mace, a hand-
> ful of parsley, cut up very fine, and two
> quarts of water, if it be a common fowl or
> duck--a turkey will require more water. Boil
> it gently for three hours, tie up a small
> bunch of thyme, and let it boil in it half an
> hour, then take it out. Thicken your soup
> with a large spoonful of butter rubbed into

---

29. Glasse, Art of Cookery, p. 129.

30. Custis, Booke of Cookery, No. 30.

two of flour, the yelks of two eggs, and
half a pint of milk. Be careful not to
let it curdle in the soup.[31]

By the time this recipe was written, Mrs. Randolph
had already earned her reputation as the best cook in
Richmond, and her preference for creamed soups probably
reflected contemporary Virginia tastes. Another new
trend--the use of tomatoes--was marked in her

VEAL SOUP.

Put into a pot three quarts of water,
three onions cut small, one spoonful of
black pepper pounded, and two of salt, with
two or three slices of lean ham; let it boil
steadily two hours longer; take out the slices
of ham, and skim off the grease if any should
rise, take a gill of good cream, mix with it
two table-spoonsful of flour very nicely, and
the yelks of two eggs beaten well, strain this
mixture, and add some chopped parsley; pour
some soup on by degrees, stir it well, and
pour it into the pot, continuing to stir until it has boiled two or three minutes to
take off the raw taste of the eggs. If the
cream be not perfectly sweet, and the eggs
quite new, the thickening will curdle in the
soup. For a change you may put a dozen ripe
tomatos in, first taking off their skins, by
letting them stand a few minutes in hot water,
when they may be easily peeled. When made in
this way you must thicken it with the flour
only. Any part of the veal may be used, but
the shin or knuckle is the nicest.[32]

---

31. Randolph, _Virginia Housewife_, pp. 18-19.

32. _Ibid._, pp. 15-16. Her recipes are the earliest
I have seen using tomatoes in soup. Amelia Simmons, _Amer-
ican Cookery_ (1796), "the first American cookbook," contains
no tomatoes whatever. Yet the Rev. William Hanbury explained in _A Complete Body of Planting and Gardening_...(2 vols.,

The special tidewater delicacy, turtle soup, required tedious preparation, but apparently everyone considered it well worth the trouble.[33]

TO DRESS TURTLE.

Kill it at night in winter, and in the morning in summer. Hang it up by the hind fins, cut off the head and let it bleed well. Separate the bottom shell from the top, with great care, lest the gall bladder be broken, which must be cautiously taken out and thrown away. Put the liver in a bowl of water. ... if there be eggs, put them also in water. It is proper to have a separate bowl of water for each article. Cut all the flesh from the bottom shell, and lay it in water; then break the shell in two, put it in a pot after having washed it clean; pour on as much water as will cover it entirely, add one pound of middling, or flitch of bacon, with four onions chopped, and set it on the fire to boil. Open the guts, cleanse them perfectly; take off the inside skin, and put them in the pot with the shell;

London, 1770-1771), II, 752-753, that the Solanum Lycopersicum, formerly cultivated as a decorative Love Apple or Mad Apple, was being used for "heightening" soups and sauces in England as well as Spain and Italy.

33. For example, when Col. James Innes, attorney general of Virginia, invited some Williamsburg friends to Richmond for a special dinner in 1790, he phrased the invitation in this way: "I arrived safely...and found all well at home, the Turtle not excepted. Tell Barraud it dies on Tuesday next and will be interr'd with the honors of War. Will you & he come up and grace his Funeral?" Innes to St. George Tucker, August 26, 1790, Tucker-Coleman Papers, College of William and Mary. CW M-1021-7.
In his enumeration of native Virginia eatables, William Byrd included several kinds of land and water turtles and commented: "The meat of all these turtles is as good as the best veal, even better, either boiled or roasted or baked, or in a ragout. I have often sampled it." Richard C. Beatty and William J. Mulloy, William Byrd's Natural History of Virginia... (Richmond, 1940), p. 86.

let them boil steadily for three hours, and
if the water boils away too much, add more.
Wash the top shell nicely after taking out
the flesh, cover it, and set it by. Parboil
the fins, clean them nicely--taking off all
the black skin, and put them in water; cut
the flesh taken from the bottom and top shell,
in small pieces; cut the fins in two, lay
them with the flesh in a dish; sprinkle some
salt over, and cover them up. When the shell,
&c. is done, take out the bacon, scrape the
shell clean, and strain the liquor; about one
quart of which must be put back in the pot;
reserve the rest for soup; pick out the guts,
and cut them in small pieces; take all the
nice bits that were strained out, put them
with the guts into the gravy; lay the fins
cut in pieces with them, and as much of the
flesh as will be sufficient to fill the upper
shell; add to it, (if a large turtle,) one
bottle of white wine; cayenne pepper, and
salt, to your taste, one gill of mushroom
catsup, one gill of lemon pickle, mace, nutmegs and cloves, pounded, to season it high.
Mix two large spoonsful of flour in one
pound and a quarter of butter; put it in
with thyme, parsley, marjoram and savory,
tied in bunches; stew all these together,
till the flesh and fins are tender; wash out
the top shell, put a puff paste around the
brim; sprinkle over the shell pepper and salt,
then take the herbs out of the stew; if the
gravy is not thick enough, add a little more
flour, and fill the shell; should there be no
eggs in the turtle, boil six new laid ones
for ten minutes, put them in cold water a
short time, peel them, cut them in two, and
place them on the turtle; make a rich forcemeat, (see receipt for forcemeat,) fry the
balls nicely, and put them also in the shell;
set it in a dripping pan, with something under
the sides to keep it steady; have the oven
heated as for bread, and let it remain in it
till nicely browned. Fry the liver and send
it in hot.

FOR THE SOUP.

At an early hour in the morning, put on
eight pounds of coarse beef, some bacon, onions,

sweet herbs, pepper and salt. Make a rich
soup, strain it and thicken with a bit of butter, and brown flour; add to it the water left
from boiling the bottom shell; season it very
high with wine, catsup, spice and cayenne; put
in the flesh you reserved, and if that is not
enough, add the nicest parts of a well boiled
calf's head; but do not use the eyes or tongue;
let it boil till tender, and serve it up with
fried forcemeat balls in it.

If you have curry powder, (see receipt for
it,) it will give a higher flavour to both
soup and turtle, than spice. Should you not
want soup, the remaining flesh may be fried,
and served with a rich gravy.[34]

Gruel was as nourishing as broth but thickened with

barley, oatmeal, or another cereal and served chiefly as

invalid food. It was sometimes made from milk instead of

broth, and sugar and spices might be added. Or it might

be thinned with wine or ale, sweetened and seasoned with

spices; this kind of mixture was called a caudle. Still

another variation--the posset--was made from hot milk

mixed with ale or wine (preferably sack or sherry) and

seasoned with sugar and spices; its body came from the

curdling effect of wine and milk heated together, without

the use of farinaceous thickening.

Porridge, once synonymous with gruel, by the seven-

teenth century had become a soft food of the consistency

of the hot cereal we serve today. Oatmeal porridge, the

Scot's staple, was prepared by stirring oatmeal into

34. Randolph, Virginia Housewife, pp. 20-22.

salted boiling water and then allowing it to bubble gently

for an hour or longer. (In Ireland it was called stir-

about.) The plum porridge associated with Christmas in

England until the end of the nineteenth century was the

ancestor of plum pudding and plum cake; in all these dishes

a plum was a dried grape. Mrs. Glasse included a tradi-

tional recipe:

> To make plumb gruel.
>
> Take two quarts of water, two large spoon-
> fuls of oatmeal, stir it together, a blade or
> two of mace, a little piece of lemon-peel;
> boil it for five or six minutes (take care it
> don't boil over) then strain it off, and put
> it into the sauce-pan again, with half a
> pound of currants clean washed and picked.
> Let them boil about ten minutes, add a glass
> of white wine, a little grated nutmeg, and
> sweeten to your palate.35

and a version suitable for company:

> To make plumb porridge for Christmas.
>
> Take a leg and shin of beef, put to them
> eight gallons of water and boil them till
> they are very tender, and when the broth is
> strong strain it out; wipe the pot and put
> in the broth again; then slice six penny
> loaves thin, cut off the top and bottom, put
> some of the liquor to it, cover it up and
> let it stand a quarter of an hour, boil it
> and strain it, and then put it into your pot.
> Let it boil a quarter of an hour, then put
> in five pounds of currants clean washed and
> picked; let them boil a little, and put in
> five pounds of raisins of the sun stoned,
> and two pounds of pruens, and let them boil
> till they swell; then put in three quarters

---

35. Glasse, <u>Art of Cookery</u>, p. 154.

of an ounce of mace, half an ounce of cloves,
two nutmegs, all of them beat fine, and mix it
with a little liquor cold, and put them in a
very little while, and take off the pot; then
put in three pounds of sugar, a little salt, a
quart of sack, a quart of claret, and the juice
of two or three lemons. You may thicken with
sego, instead of bread, if you please; pour
them into earthen pans, and keep them for use.
You must boil two pounds of pruens in a quart
of water till they are tender, and strain them
into the pot, when it is a-boiling.[36]

In eighteenth-century cookery, distinctions among
broth, soup, gruel, porridge and pottage were not clearly
defined. Pottage, once a highly composite stew that might
contain any variety of ingredients boiled together in the
same pot, was beginning to take its character from the
French potage and becoming a soup of any kind; in the next
century it would disappear from the menu. But the pease
porridge of the ancient nursery rhyme was still being prepared and served much like modern split pea soup.[37] Mrs.
Custis's White Broth, on the other hand, was really a
dessert pudding:

Take a capon with whole mace, cloves sina-
mon, & boyle cur[rants] & raysons in a cloth,
& when your broth is enough take out your capon
& put in as much cream as will make it white
then blanch & beat almonds & strayne them with
cream, then beat & strayne as many eggs as will
make it thick enough, put in a little sack &

---

36. Ibid., p. 122.

37. For examples see Ibid., pp. 124, 125; Custis,
Booke of Cookery, No. 31, 32.

set all on a slow fire, & keepe it stiring
till it is thick enough.[38]

Though vegetables were ignored in the early cookbooks except when they were used as garnishes or ingredients in made dishes, by the end of the century they were
receiving individual attention and sometimes appearing in
continental dress--French, Spanish, Dutch, German. Mrs.
Glasse offered a bit of succinct advice "concerning garden things":

> Most people spoil garden things by over-
> boiling them. All things that are green should
> have a little crispness, for if they are over-
> boiled they neither have any sweetness or beauty.[39]

Her root vegetables were usually boiled, drained and served
with a seasoned sauce or brown gravy; or else they were
mashed or chopped, seasoned and reheated. Sauces and gravies were thickened with eggs or cream, and seasonings
included chopped onions, herbs, spices, wine and vinegar.

Boiled asparagus dressed the English way, for example,
was served on toast with melted butter alongside in a boat
--to relieve guests of the annoyance of greasy fingers;
dressed the Spanish way, it was reheated in oil and vinegar,
with the option of added garlic; the French way, with a
sauce of egg yolks and vinegar prepared separately, like

---

38. Custis, Booke of Cookery, No. 203.

39. Glasse, Art of Cookery, p. 18.

modern hollandaise. Windsor beans dressed the German
way were cooked in a tightly covered saucepan with parsley, chopped onions, and a pound of butter but no water.
Red cabbage dressed the Dutch way was chopped, boiled,
drained, then returned to the stewpan with chopped onion,
butter, and vinegar diluted with water, and allowed to
simmer until all the liquid was absorbed.[40]

Only Mrs. Randolph devoted an entire section of her
book to vegetables, a chapter of practical advice about
choosing them, preparing, cooking and serving them.[41]
All fresh vegetables, in her opinion, ought to be picked
early in the morning of the day they are to be used; they
should be young and tender--not the largest and most ma-
ture specimens dear to the gardener's heart. Leafy varieties should be thoroughly washed and carefully picked
over. For most things the less water they are boiled in,
the better, and, like Mrs. Glasse, Mrs. Randolph repeatedly warned against overcooking. Finally, she preferred
to drain the vegetables carefully and serve them immediately with butter or a very simple sauce. For root vegetables (carrots, Jerusalem artichokes, turnips, beets,
parsnips, potatoes, salsify) she recommended boiling them

---

40. Ibid., pp. 15-18, 343-344; Bradley, British
Housewife, p. 432.

41. Randolph, Virginia Housewife, pp. 95-113.

whole and emphasized the importance of choosing those of

uniform size for more even cooking and attractive appearance.

Where Mrs. Bradley and Mrs. Glasse used European reci-

pes to give their books an up-to-date tone, Mrs. Randolph

featured the Virginia way and included native vegetables

not commonly served in England. Turnip tops, she declared,

"are still better boiled with bacon in the Virginia style:

if fresh and young, they will be done in about twenty

minutes--drain them on the back of a sieve, and put them

under the bacon."[42] As for field peas:

> There are many varieties of these peas;
> the smaller kind are the most delicate. Have
> them young and newly gathered, shell and boil
> them tender; pour them in a colander to drain;
> put some lard in a frying pan; when it boils,
> mash the peas, and fry them in a cake of a
> light brown; put it in the dish with the crust
> uppermost--garnish with thin bits of fried
> bacon. They are very nice when fried whole,
> so that each pea is distinct from the other;
> but they must be boiled less, and fried with
> great care. Plain boiling is a very common
> way of dressing them.[43]

Other native vegetables for which she recommended

boiling, before the addition of seasonings and dressings,

were sweet potatoes, pumpkin, squash, and tomatoes.[44]

---

42. _Ibid._, pp. 103-104.

43. _Ibid._, p. 111.

44. Though corn meal is often used in Mrs. Randolph's recipes, green corn does not appear either as roasting ears or boiled or stewed or as corn pudding.
Yet Virginians valued roasting ears to such an

Her European dishes were largely Spanish, introduced

apparently for their tomatoes, as in <u>olla</u>, <u>gaspacho</u> and

<u>ropa vieja</u>.[45]

The "stewed" fruits in the recipe books were usually

preserves or ingredients in sweet desserts that we would

call puddings today. A typical example is Mrs. Randolph's

apple custard:

> Pare and core twelve pippins, slice them
> tolerably thick, put a pound of loaf sugar in
> a stew pan, with a pint of water and twelve
> cloves: boil and skim it, then put in the
> apples, and stew them till clear, and but
> little of the syrup remains--lay them in a
> deep dish, and take out the cloves; when the
> apples are cold, pour in a quart of rich
> boiled custard--set it in water, and make it
> boil till the custard is set--take care the
> water does not get into it.[46]

Even so, almost any fruit or berry could be heated

with sugar and spice and served either hot or cold as a

compote, a suitable dessert for family and guests. When

---

extent that Jefferson cultivated Indian corn in his Paris
garden "to eat green in our manner." Jefferson to Nicholas
Lewis, Sept. 17, 1787, in Edwin M. Betts, ed., <u>Thomas Jefferson's Garden Book, 1766-1824</u> (Philadelphia, 1944), p.130.
Apparently the delicacy was borrowed from the Indians who,
according to Beverley, "delight much to feed on Roasting-
ears; that is, the Indian Corn, gathered green and milky,
before it is grown to its full bigness, and roasted before
the Fire, in the Ear." Robert Beverley, <u>The History and
Present State of Virginia</u>, ed. by Louis B. Wright (Chapel
Hill, 1947), p. 180.

45. <u>Ibid</u>., pp. 83, 89.

46. <u>Ibid</u>., p. 118.

Jefferson in Paris began to entertain the world's gourmets, he made a list of desserts fashionable at the French court. Along with pastries, custards, cakes and fritters, he included a variety of fruit compotes: pears, cherries, strawberries, oranges and apples.[47] Yet none of these fruits appeared in his collection of recipes--perhaps for the same reason that they are not to be found in English cookbooks: no directions are needed for their preparation. Mrs. Randolph offered one exception:

COMPOTE OF APPLES.

Pare and core the apples, and if you prefer it, cut them in four, wash them clean, and put them in a pan with water and sugar enough to cover them; add cinnamon and lemon peel, which has been previously soaked, scraped on the inside, and cut in strings; boil them gently until the apples are done, take them out in a deep dish, boil the syrup to a proper consistency, and pour it on them: it will take a pound of sugar for a large dish.[48]

Perhaps because of Queen Anne's personal appearance and appetite, her era is sometimes satirized as "the Pudding Age." But the heavy English boiled pudding of tradition was already going out of style at the end of the seventeenth century, when the French satirist François Maximilien Misson wrote his famous description of it:

---

47. Marie Kimball, ed., Thomas Jefferson's Cook Book (Richmond, 1949), p. 35.

48. Randolph, Virginia Housewife, p. 128.

> The _Pudding_ is a Dish very difficult to
> be describ'd, because of the several Sorts
> there are of it; Flower, Milk, Eggs, Butter,
> Sugar, Suet, Marrow, Raisins, &c., &c., are
> the most common Ingredients of a _Pudding_.
> They bake them in an Oven, they boil them
> with Meat, they make them fifty several Ways:
> BLESSED BE HE THAT INVENTED PUDDING, for it
> is a Manna that hits the Palates of all Sorts
> of People; a Manna better than that of the
> Wilderness, because the People are never weary
> of it. Ah, what an excellent Thing is an
> _English_ _Pudding_! _To_ _come_ _in_ _Pudding_ _time_, is
> as much as to say, to come in the most lucky
> Moment in the World.[49]

The most popular member of this large family of pud-

dings was the plum pudding, which survives today. The

traditional ingredients are: meat or fowl minced; suet

or marrow chopped; spices and sugar; raisins, currants,

and almonds beaten to a paste; grated bread crumbs or

Naples bicuit; eggs to hold it together and supply limited

leavening; wine or brandy for additional flavor. These

ingredients were thoroughly mixed, then tied in a floured

cloth and boiled several hours.[50]

Then, there were traditional blood puddings, in

which blood from the animal or fowl was substituted for

the minced meat, and oatmeal, or some other form of groats,

---

49. From his dictionary of curious things in London,
1698, published later in translation as _Observations of a_
Traveller, quoted in John Ashton, _Social Life in the Reign_
of Queen Anne... (2 vols., London, 1882), I, 188-189.

50. For a delicious modern adaptation see Helen
Bullock, _The Williamsburg Art of Cookery_... (Williamsburg,
1939), pp. 252-253.

for the bread crumbs.[51] Instead of being wrapped in a
cloth, these "black puddings" or "hog puddings" were
usually stuffed into sausage cases prepared earlier from
animal intestines, preferably those of hogs.[52]

Already in Queen Anne's day English tastes were
beginning to favor lighter puddings in greater variety.
Flour replaced bread crumbs or oatmeal, and cream and
butter were used instead of suet or marrow to produce a
batter, which might be boiled in a cloth or baked.[53]
Small boiled puddings similar to dumplings were becoming
more popular, as was the hasty pudding made in a saucepan
and often served cold, like modern pudding.

The cookbooks, of course, reflected changing tastes.
Mrs. Smith's chapter on puddings, for example, runs to
twenty-two pages; Mrs. Glasse's, twenty years later, has
only four pages on puddings, but her rules take into
account all the kinds popular at mid-century:

> Rules to be observed in making puddings, &c.
>
> In boiled puddings, take great care the
> bag or cloth be very clean, not soapy, but

---

51. A groat was also a coin worth four pence;
hence the double pun in the proverb "Blood without groats
[family without fortune] is nought."

52. For recipes see Glasse, Art of Cookery, pp.
249-250; Bradley, British Housewife, pp. 437-438; Harrison, Pocket-book, p. 53.

53. Baked in pastry "coffins," they became custard
pies; see below pp. 126-127.

dipped in hot water, and well floured. If
a bread pudding, tie it loose; if a batter-
pudding, tie it close, and be sure the water
boils when you put the pudding in, and you
should move the puddings in the pot now and
then, for fear they stick. When you make a
batter-pudding, first mix the flour well with
a little milk, then put in the ingredients by
degrees, and it will be smooth and not have
lumps; but for a plain batter-pudding, the
best way is to strain it through a coarse hair
sieve, that it may neither have lumps, nor the
treadles of the eggs: and all other puddings,
strain the eggs when they are beat. If you
boil them in wooden bowls, or china dishes,
butter the inside before you put in your batter; and for all baked puddings, butter the
pan or dish before the pudding is put in.[54]

Mrs. Custis's choices represent a good balance between

the old and the new in Queen Anne's time. Her baked pud-

dings included marrow, almond, rice, and curd; if they were

baked in pastry shells, she labeled them pies. Of the

fourteen boiled puddings in her collection, half were the

heavy, old-fashioned kind made with bread crumbs or oatmeal;

one was a goose blood pudding, boiled in the skin of the

neck; one was a haggis; one a conventional liver pudding;

three were batters boiled in a cloth; two were prepared in

a stewpan. Of the two hasty puddings, one was the conven-

tional frumenty:

Take 3 pintes of new milke & one pinte of
creame, and boyle it with a flake or 2 of mace
& some nutmegg, & then put in your wheat, &

---

54. Glasse, Art of Cookery, p. 133; cf. Bradley,
British Housewife, pp. 58-60.

keepe it boyling & stirring, & then thicken it
with eggs well beaten, or wheat flower & put
in some raysons of the sun beeing before plumpt,
& streyne in some saffron if you please, & sweet-
en it well with sugar, & soe serve it up.[55]

Her boiled dumplings, too, were conventional:

To make white Puddings.

Take 3 pintes of milke & when it is
boyled put in two quarts of great oatmeale
bruised a little, & stirr it over the fire
till it be ready to boyle then take it of &
cover it close all night, 3 pound of suet
minced small put in with 3 grated nutmeggs
the youlks of 8 eggs 2 whites & a little rose-
water, a pound of sugar & a little grated
bread currans & creame as you think fit, this
quantety will make 3 or 4 dosin.[56]

A comparison with Virginia tastes at the end of the

century may be found in Mrs. Randolph's version of plum

pudding, her boiled loaf, dumplings and Indian pudding.

Her plum pudding contained suet, spice, currants and rai-

sins and it was boiled in a cloth for eight hours; but

it was lighter in texture because flour replaced bread

crumbs and the sugar was powdered.[57] Her boiled loaf,

on the other hand, was quite traditional:

Pour a quart of boiling milk over four
little rolls of bread--cover them up, turning
them occasionally till saturated with the
milk; tie them very tight in cloths, and boil
them an hour; lay them in the dish, and pour

---

55. Custis, Booke of Cookery, No. 100.

56. Ibid., No. 80.

57. Randolph, Virginia Housewife, pp. 119-120.

a little melted butter over them; for sauce,
have butter in a boat, seasoned with wine,
sugar, and grated nutmeg.[58]

Her dumplings, bearing the old name, were made in the new

style:

A NICE BOILED PUDDING.

Make up a pint of flour at sun rise, exactly as you do for bread; see that it rises well
--have a large pot of water boiling; and half
an hour before the puddings are to go to table,
make the dough in balls, the size of a goose
egg; throw them in the water, and boil them
quickly, keeping the pot covered: they must
be torn asunder, as cutting will make them
heavy; eat them with powdered sugar, butter,
and grated nutmeg.[59]

And her boiled Indian Pudding was wholly American:

Mix one quart of corn meal, with three
quarts of milk; take care it be not lumpy--
add three eggs and a gill of molasses; it
must be put on at sun rise, to eat at three
o'clock; the great art in this pudding is
tying the bag properly, as the meal swells
very much.[60]

---

58. Ibid., p. 118.

59. Ibid., pp. 125-126.

60. Ibid., p. 127.

IV. COOKING METHODS: ROASTING, BROILING, FRYING

For "roasting meat to perfection" the cook had to pay proper attention to four things: the cleanliness of her equipment, the quality of her fire, the distance of her meat from the fire, and frequent basting.[1]

First, from her collection of spits of various lengths, she chose one suitable for the piece of meat to be roasted. If it had been carefully scrubbed with sand and water and thoroughly dried before it was put away after the last use, nothing further had to be done to it now. But if it had rusted from neglect or been covered with a heavy coat of oil or grease to prevent rusting, it would have to be cleaned again, for the flavor of the meat would be spoiled by rust or rancid oil.

The fire had to be clear and brisk, regardless of the size of the roast. It was necessary, therefore, to make it up well in advance and regulate it so that a

1. Summary from Martha Bradley, The British House-wife... (London, [c. 1770]), pp. 32-33; [Hannah Glasse], The Art of Cookery... (7th edn., London, 1760), pp. 1-2, 12; Sarah Harrison, The House-keeper's Pocket-book... (6th edn., London, 1755), p. 13; Elizabeth Raffald, The Experienced English House-keeper... (4th edn., London, 1775), p. 53; Mary Randolph, The Virginia Housewife... (Philadelphia, 1855), p. 26.

suitable bed of embers would be ready for use at the proper time.[2] The proper place on the hearth was important, too--a roaring fire spread all over the hearth was good for nothing but overheating the room and the cook. The roasting fire was a small one in the spot where the spit was to be suspended between the firedogs, preferably near the front of the fireplace and to one side; the spit had to be turned, and the dripping-pan must be accessible for convenient basting.

The first requirement for a good roasting fire was that it be "clear at the bottom." Half-way through the roasting of a large piece of meat it was usually necessary to "move the dripping-pan and spit a little from the fire, and stir up a good brisk fire; for according to the goodness of your fire, your meat will be done sooner or later."[3] For a fowl or small cut of meat "a pretty little brisk fire" is desirable so "that it may be done quick and nice" because a bird cooked slowly "will not eat near so sweet, or look so beautiful to the eye."[4] On the other hand, if the fire is too hot, "the meat is scorched, the

---

2. Mrs. Bradley, British Housewife, p. 33, directed that the fire "be made up in Time" and that it be "proportioned to the Service."

3. Glasse, Art of Cookery, pp. 1-2.

4. Ibid., pp. 1, 14.

outside is hard, and prevents the heat from penetrating into the meat, and will appear enough before it be little more than half done."[5]

Only experience could dictate the proper distance between the meat and bed of coals to produce even roasting. Most spit dogs were fitted with hooks at intervals all along their height, so that the spit could be moved up and down on the dogs as well as forward and backward in relation to the fire. In Mrs. Randolph's opinion, a mechanical jack was greatly to be desired, but a skilled hand turning the spit "before a steady clear fire" would ensure an even distribution of the heat.[6]

Proper basting was important for flavor, texture, and appearance. Most authorities agreed that meat should never be salted before being placed on the spit because salt "draws out all the gravy."[7] For this reason salt was added to the liquid in the dripping pan along with butter or lard--and water if the roast was very large. Frequent basting kept the meat moist and so speeded up the cooking

---

5. Raffald, English House-keeper, p. 53.

6. Randolph, Virginia Housewife, p. 27. She recommended another piece of roasting equipment in common use for roasting birds, apples, potatoes--the tin Dutch oven, shaped like half a cylinder and equipped with a spit; see Chapter II for an illustration.

7. Glasse, Art of Cookery, p. 2.

process, but too much basting could spoil the appearance
of the joint. "Beef may look brown," Mrs. Randolph explained, "but the whiter the other meats are, the more
genteel are they and if properly roasted, they may be
perfectly done, and quite white." Half boiling a joint
before spitting it was considered a barbarism because it
destroyed the fine flavor.[8] Instead, a good cook covered
the tops of large cuts with thickly buttered paper and
set them "a good Way from the Fire"[9] for part of the cooking time, while she basted over the paper. Veal and lamb
required paper only for the fat, and fowls only for the
breast. A pork loin or a whole pig did not require paper
at all, for it could be roasted with the skin on; indeed,
this treatment was preferred because the skin could be
scored across to make better crackling. Just before serving a joint it was customary to dredge it in flour and
turn it quickly a few times "to make a fine froth."[10]

There was general agreement about roasting time:
For mutton or veal a six-pound leg required an hour; a
large saddle, three hours because it was papered; a breast,

---

8. Randolph, _Virginia Housewife_, p. 27.

9. Harrison, _Pocket-book_, p. 14.

10. _Ibid._, pp. 13-17; Bradley, _British Housewife_,
pp. 33-36; Glasse, _Art of Cookery_, pp. 2, 3, 12, 13;
Randolph, _Virginia Housewife_, p. 26.

half an hour. For a thick cut of beef weighing twenty
pounds, three hours was adequate. Pork ought to be well
done, and the rule was fifteen minutes per pound. Fowls
varied by size, rather than kind: twenty minutes for a
small chicken, forty-five for a turkey or goose, ten for
a small bird. Mrs. Bradley offered a rule of thumb:
"When the Steam from the Meat is drawn toward the fire,
'tis a Sign it is near done."[11]

Forcemeat stuffings of various kinds were commonly
used inside fowls, large fish, rabbits, pigs--anything
roasted whole, with a natural cavity to be filled. While
most recipes specified the use of a spit, there were other
ways of cooking stuffed articles. Mrs. Glasse in one in-
stance recommended a string suspended from a pothanger or
a high spit:

> To roast a fowl with chestnuts.
>
> First take some chestnuts, roast them very
> carefully, so as not to burn them, take off
> the skin, and peel them, take about a dozen
> of them cut small, and bruise them in a mortar;
> parboil the liver of the fowl, bruise it, cut
> about a quarter of a pound of ham or bacon,
> and pound it; then mix them all together, with
> a good deal of parsley chopped fine, a little
> sweet herbs, some mace, pepper, salt, and nut-
> meg; mix these together and put into your fowl,
> and roast it. The best way of doing it is to
> tie the neck, and hang it up by the legs to
> roast with a string, and baste it with butter.
> For sauce take the rest of the chestnuts peeled

---

11. Bradley, _British Housewife_, p. 34.

and skinned, put them into some good gravy,
with a little white wine, and thicken it with
a piece of butter rolled in flour; than take
up your fowl, lay it in the dish, and pour in
the sauce. Garnish with lemon.[12]

Mrs. Smith suggested two ways to roast a large fish--

on a spit or in the embers:

Take a large Pike, gut it and clean it,
and lard it with Eel and Bacon, as you lard a
Fowl; then take Thyme and Savory, Salt, Mace,
and Nutmeg, some Crumbs of Bread, Beef-suet
and Parsley; shred all very fine, and mix it
up with raw Eggs; make it in a long Pudding,
and put it in the Belly of your Pike, skewer
up the Belly, and dissolve Anchovies in Butter,
and baste it with it; put two Splints on each
Side of the Pike, and tie it to the Spit; melt
Butter thick for the Sauce, or, if you please,
Oyster-sauce, and bruise the Pudding in it.
Garnish with Lemon.[13]

To roast a Pike in Embers.

When your fish is scal'd, and well dry'd
in a cloth, make a pudding with sweet herbs,
grated bread, and onion, wrapt up in butter;
put it into the belly, and sew it up, turn
the tail into the mouth, and roll it up in
white Paper, and then in brown, wet them both,
and tye them round with packthread; then rake
it up in the Embers, and let it lie two or
three hours, then take it up, and take the
pudding out of the belly, mix it with the
sauce, such as is usually made for fish, and
serve it up.[14]

---

12. Glasse, <u>Art of Cookery</u>, p. 72; cf. her treatment of pigeon, p. 6.

13. E. Smith, <u>The Compleat Housewife</u>... (Williamsburg, 1742), p. 11.

14. <u>Ibid</u>. (11th edn., London, 1742), p. 18--an
example of Parks's failure to include a recipe suitable
for use in Virginia kitchens.

Mrs. Randolph's Virginia specialty required a plank:

TO ROAST A SHAD.

Fill the cavity with good forcemeat, sew
it up, and tie it on a board of proper size,
cover it with bread crumbs, with some salt and
pepper, set it before the fire to roast; when
done on one side, turn it, tie it again, and
when sufficiently done, pull out the thread,
and serve it up with butter and parsley poured
over it.[15]

Though there were few variations in the roasting

process and finished roasts were usually placed on the

platter with a simple garnish, discriminating guests might

find diversity in the accompanying sauces served in sepa-

rate sauce boats.[16] A few combinations were conventional:

for fowls, a white sauce, bread sauce, egg, mushroom, or

celery sauce; for lamb, mint sauce; for ducks, orange or

onion sauce; for fish, either oyster, lobster, or shrimp

sauce; for a goose and for pork, applesauce or onion; for

a green goose, gooseberries and sorrel juice added to a

simple butter sauce; for venison, something sweet-sour,

like melted currant jelly, or red wine and sugar, or vine-

gar and sugar.

The following recipes illustrate interesting varia-

tions. Mrs. Glasse's general directions for roasting pork:

---

15. Randolph, Virginia Housewife, p. 59.

16. For sauce recipes see below pp. 135-147.

Pork must be well done, or it is apt to surfeit. When you roast a loin, take a sharp penknife and cut the skin across, to make the crackling eat the better. The chine you must not cut at all. The best way to roast a leg, is first to parboil it, then skin it and roast it; baste it with butter, then take a little sage, shred it fine, a little pepper and salt, a little nutmeg, and a few crumbs of bread; throw these over it all the time it is roasting, then have a little drawn gravy to put in the dish with the crumbs that drop from it. Some love the knuckle stuffed with onion and sage shred small, with a little pepper and salt, gravy and apple-sauce to it. This they call a mock-goose. The spring, or hand of pork, if very young, roasted like a pig, eats very well, otherwise it is better boiled. The sparerib should be basted with a little bit of butter, a very little dust of flour, and some sage shred small: but we never make any sauce to it but apple-sauce. The best way to dress pork griskins is to roast them, baste them with a little butter and crumbs of bread, sage, and a little pepper and salt. Few eat any thing with these but mustard.[17]

And:

To roast a pig with the skin on.

Let your pig be newly killed, draw him, flea[18] him, and wipe him very dry with a cloth; then make a hard meat with a pint of cream, the yolks of six eggs, grated bread, and beef sewet, seasoned with salt, pepper, mace, nutmeg, thyme, and lemon-peel; make of this a pretty stiff pudding, stuff the belly of the pig, and sew it up; then spit it, and lay it down to roast. Let your dripping-pan be very clean, then pour into it a pint of red wine, grate some nutmeg all over it, then throw a little salt over, a little thyme, and some lemon-peel minced; when it is enough shake a

---

17. Glasse, _Art of Cookery_, p. 3.

18. I.e., flay him--score the skin in strips.

little flour over it, and baste it with butter,
to have a fine froth. Take it up and lay it in
a dish, cut off the head, take the sauce which
is in your dripping-pan, and thicken it with a
piece of butter; then take the brains, bruise
them, mix them with the sauce, rub in a little
dried sage, pour it into your dish, and serve
it up. Garnish with hard eggs cut into quarters, and if you have not sauce enough add half
a pint of good gravy.

Note, You must take great care no ashes
fall into the dripping-pan, which may be prevented by having a good fire, which will not
want any stirring.[19]

Mrs. Custis recommended a simpler procedure:

To roste A Pigg.

When the pigg is halfe rosted pull of the
scinn & stick it full of sprigs of time, &
baste it with butter & crumbs of bread till it
be enough. for the sauce take grated bread &
water a little vinegar nutmegg & sugar & boyle
all these together, then put in some butter &
serve them up.[20]

She preferred to serve her fish sauce on the fish, thus:

To roste A carpe.

First salt the carpe then wash it very well
& take out all the insyde of it, & fill the
belly of the carpe with grated bread & a pritty
deale of time minced very small, & put in halfe
a pound of fresh butter, then sow up the belly
& ty it to the spit with 2 laths, for an houre
in which time it will be roasted, then rip up
the belly & let out the sauce & mingle it with
some more melted butter & some minced leamon &
capers mingle all well together, then pour it
on your carpe being laide in a handsome dish,
& garnish it with ginger.[21]

---

19. Glasse, Art of Cookery, p. 64.

20. Frances Parke Custis, A Booke of Cookery, No. 42.

21. Ibid., No. 188.

Sturgeon--too large to roast whole--was treated like a joint of meat:

> To roast a piece of fresh sturgeon.
>
> Get a piece of fresh sturgeon, of about eight or ten pounds, let it lay in water and salt six or eight hours, with its scales on; then fasten it on the spit, and baste it well with butter for a quarter of an hour, then with a little flour, then grate a nutmeg all over it, a little mace and pepper beaten fine, and salt thrown over it, and a few sweet herbs dried and powdered fine, and then crumbs of bread; then keep basting a little, and drudging with crumbs of bread, and with what falls from it till it is enough. In the mean time prepare this sauce: take a pint of water, an anchovy, a little piece of lemon-peel, an onion, a bundle of sweet herbs, mace, cloves, whole pepper, black and white, a little piece of horse-raddish; cover it close, let it boil a quarter of an hour, then strain it, put it into the sauce-pan again, pour in a pint of white wine, about a dozen oysters and the liquor, two spoonfuls of catchup, two of wal-nut-pickle, the inside of a crab bruised fine, or lobster, shrimps or prawns, a good piece of butter rolled in flour, a spoonful of mushroom-pickle, or juice of lemon. Boil it all together; when your fish is enough, lay it in your dish and pour the sauce over it. Garnish with fried toasts and lemon.[22]

Lobsters, on the other hand, were not often large enough to allow a spit to be thrust through their bodies. Mrs. Harrison's alternative method suggested that they be tied to the spit for roasting, and Mrs. Glasse permitted parboiling first--"as good a way to the full as roasting

---

22. Glasse, Art of Cookery, pp. 180-181.

them, and not half the trouble."[23]

Mrs. Custis's roast capon called for a simple oyster dressing:

> Take a fat capon & pull & draw it then
> stuff the body with raw oysters, then truss &
> lay it to the fire, & set a clean dish under
> it to save the gravie, then make the sauce for
> it, with water that cometh from the oysters, &
> a little clarret, a little pepper & vinegar &
> the gravie, & rub an ounion up & downe the
> sauce, that it may taste well of it, when it
> hath boyled a little put in some butter & mince
> in some leamon and leamon pill, then serve it
> up with slyced leamon on the capon & round
> about the dish.[24]

And for elegant service Mrs. Glasse recommended an all-purpose recipe:

> To dress a turky or fowl to perfection.
>
> Bone them, and make a force-meat thus:
> take the flesh of a fowl, cut it small, then
> take a pound of veal, beat it in a mortar,
> with half a pound of beef sewet, as much
> crumbs of bread, some mushrooms, truffles and
> morels cut small, a few sweet herbs and pars-
> ley, with some nutmeg, pepper, and salt, a
> little mace beaten, some lemon-peel cut fine;
> mix all these together, with the yolks of two
> eggs, then fill your turky, and roast it.
> This will do for a large turky, and so in pro-
> portion for a fowl. Let your sauce be good
> gravy, with mushrooms, truffles and morels in
> it: then garnish with lemon, and for variety
> sake you may lard your fowl or turky.[25]

---

23. Harrison, Pocket-book, p. 14; Glasse, Art of Cookery, p. 185.

24. Custis, Booke of Cookery, No. 37.

25. Glasse, Art of Cookery, p. 70.

BROILING

To a modern Englishwoman, to broil is to grill. In
the eighteenth century it meant to cook on a gridiron, an
arrangement of parallel iron bars--usually seven of them--
in a frame, standing on short legs and equipped with a
long handle. It was placed either directly over the bed
of coals or upon a brandreth (an iron trivet or tripod
with longer legs).[26]

The importance of broiling as a culinary art Mrs.
Bradley expressed in these words:

> Broiling may very well be considered as
> an additional Article to Roasting. It is of
> the same Kind, the naked Fire being used, and
> the Difference being more in the Instrument
> than any Thing else: It is one of the small-
> est Articles in Cookery, but we propose to omit
> nothing. The Advantage of Roasting above Broil-
> ing is plain, because it is out of the Way of
> the Smoak; whereas broiled Things are exposed
> to it, if there be ever so little. It is for
> this Reason that most of those Things we usually
> broil, eat better roasted: However, as there
> are some real Uses of this Way of Cookery, and
> some very good Dishes prepared by it, we shall
> here give the needful Directions of doing it
> well, as on the other Occasions. Cleanliness
> is an essential here, as in any Article of
> Cookery: and the briskness and clearness of
> the Fire is half the Matter; it depends upon
> four Things, a clear Fire, a clean Gridiron, a
> quick Eye to watch, and a ready Hand to turn.
> Very frequent turning is necessary to some
> Things, and very little to others; this we

---

26. Recipes reading "to grill" require the use of
a salamander.

shall shew under the several Heads: But the great Article is to watch the Time of their being properly done.

As the having Things hot that are broiled is a great Article of their Value, the Cook should always set a Dish to heat as soon as she lays on the Thing to broil; and she must never hasten in any Manner any thing whatever that is broiling, it only makes Smoak and a mischievous Flame. These are all the general Directions needful to broiling. We come now to the Particulars.[27]

Mrs. Glasse's directions for broiling beef steaks

described the method in exact detail:

To broil steaks.

First have a very clear brisk fire; let your gridiron be very clean; put it on the fire, and take a chaffing-dish with a few hot coals out of the fire. Put the dish on it which is to lay your steaks on, then take fine rump steaks about half an inch thick; put a little pepper and salt on them, lay them on the gridiron, and (if you like it) take a shallot or two, or a fine onion and cut it fine; put it into your dish. Don't turn your steaks till one side is done, then when you turn the other side there will soon be a fine gravy lie on top of the steak, which you must be careful not to lose. When the steaks are enough, take them carefully off into your dish, that none of the gravy be lost; then have ready a hot dish and cover, and carry them hot to table, with the cover on.[28]

Both Mrs. Bradley and Mrs. Glasse proposed slight

variations in method for broiling mutton and pork, either

chops or steaks. For these the gridiron should be raised

---

27. Bradley, British Housewife, p. 40.

28. Glasse, Art of Cookery, p. 7.

higher from the coals so that they might cook more slowly
and thoroughly; they should be turned frequently and
quickly "because of their Fat"--that is to say, it is
more important to have the fat well done than to preserve
the gravy.[29] Mrs. Glasse further warned against trying
to "baste any thing on a gridiron, for it only makes it
smoaked and burnt."[30]

It was agreed that pigeons, small fowls and birds
might be broiled whole or split into halves, but apparently everyone preferred to roast them on a spit. Cooks
expressed a similar attitude toward fish, offering a few
recipes for broiling it but often advising that it be
boiled first.[31]

In Mrs. Randolph's Virginia, broiling methods were
essentially the same. She, too, emphasized the importance
of serving broiled food as hot as possible, "immediately
from the gridiron."[32] Her broiled shad, when compared with
her planked shad, points up conventional distinctions:

TO BROIL A SHAD.

Separate one side from the back-bone, so
that it will lie open without being split in

---

29. Ibid., pp. 6, 7, 8, 75; Bradley, British Housewife, p. 41. Note that Mrs. Custis has no broiling recipes.

30. Glasse, Art of Cookery, p. 8.

31. For examples, see ibid., pp. 171-176.

32. Randolph, Virginia Housewife, p. 33.

two; wash it clean, dry it with a cloth, sprinkle some salt and pepper on it, and let it stand till you are ready to broil it; have the gridiron hot and well greased, broil it nicely, and pour over it melted butter.[33]

FRYING

There is a tradition that a good Southern cook can prepare an entire meal with a frying pan and that it was ever thus. On the contrary, the iron pot was the essential piece of equipment in colonial kitchens, and fried food was no more elegant then than it is now. The contemporary attitude was stated by Mrs. Bradley:

> After broiling we are to mention frying, though little need be said about it. It is a coarse and greasy Kind of Cookery, in Fashion in the Country, where there are great Appetites and strong Stomachs, but is at present entirely left off in genteel Families, except for nice Things, and in a particular Manner; these we shall shew how to dress in their proper Places, but we here treat only of plain frying. As nothing shall be omitted that can be useful to a Servant in any Rank or Condition, we here give the Rules for doing this. Frying Meat answers the Purpose of broiling, but not so well; the Heat of the Dish is a great Matter, so that there must always be a Chafing-dish of Coals ready to set it over, that the Meat may be put into it hot. Let the Frying-Pan be clean, and the Fire brisk and clear, for Smoak will get in if there be any.[34]

Among the "nice Things" that could be fried, she

---

33. *Ibid.*, p. 59.

34. Bradley, *British Housewife*, p. 42.

included beef steaks prepared in this "particular Manner":

> Let the Steaks be cut thinner than for
> broiling, and when a Dish is set over a
> Chafing dish of Coals, shred an Onion into
> it with a very little Water; put a Piece of
> Butter into the Pan, and when it is melted
> put in the Steaks peppered and salted; when
> done a little, turn them, and repeat this as
> Occasion requires. Finally, add a very little
> Flour, and then put them into the Dish. Some
> fry the Onion with the Steak, but this makes
> it stronger.[35]

Mrs. Randolph recommended special care in the

dredging process: "Fish, and all other articles for fry-

ing, after being nicely prepared, should be laid on a

board and dredged with flour or meal mixed with salt;

when it becomes dry on one side, turn it, and dredge the

other."[36] She, too, restricted her use of the frying pan

to slices of beef, cutlets of veal and pork, Scotch col-

lops; to small fish, oysters, sturgeon cutlets and roe.

At the same time, she introduced an innovation now famous

as a traditional Southern dish:

FRIED CHICKENS.

> Cut them up as for the fricassee, dredge
> them well with flour, sprinkle them with salt,
> put them into a good quantity of boiling lard,
> and fry them a light brown; fry small pieces
> of mush and a quantity of parsley nicely picked,
> to be served in the dish with the chickens,
> take half a pint of rich milk, add to it a

---

35. Ibid., p. 43; cf. Harrison, Pocket-book, p. 22,
using onions and adding claret or beer to the gravy.

36. Randolph, Virginia Housewife, pp. 27-28.

small bit of butter, with pepper, salt, and
chopped parsley; stew it a little, and pour
it over the chickens, and then garnish with
the fried parsley.[37]

Mrs. Custis fried only sausages and soles, and these

were partly stewed:

To fry Soles.

First gut your soles, & wash or wipe them
clean, then fry them well in hoggs larde, &
when they are fryed take out the longer bones
that goes downe the back, & you must have some
anchovis made ready before, with theyr scinns
taken of, & theyr back bones pulled out, then
put them in the places from whence the back
bones were taken of the soles, and squeese into them some juice of leamon or orringe, soe
stew them over the coles in a dish, with white
wine, verges, water, & butter.[38]

Mrs. Glasse fried fish, tripe, beef steaks, and

thin strips of loin of lamb in similar ways. Her direc-

tions for fish gave special attention to the problem of

avoiding the greasy effect so deplored by Mrs. Bradley:

Observe always in the frying of any sort
of fish; first, that you dry your fish very
well in a clean cloth, then flour it. Let
your stew-pan you fry them in be very nice
and clean, and put in as much beef dripping,
or hog's lard, as will almost cover your fish;
and be sure it boils before you put in your
fish. Let it fry quick, and let it be of a
fine light brown, but not too dark a colour.
Have your fish-slice ready, and if there is
occasion turn it: when it is enough, take it
up, and lay a coarse cloth on a dish, on

---

37. *Ibid.*, pp. 75-76.

38. Custis, Booke of Cookery, No. 194; see also
No. 25.

which lay your fish to drain all the grease
from it; if you fry parsley do it quick, and
take great care to whip it out of the pan so
good as it is crisp, or it will lose its fine
colour. Take great care that your dripping
be very nice and clean....
    Some love fish in batter; then you must
beat an egg fine, and dip your fish in just
as you are going to put it in the pan; or as
good a batter as any, is a little ale and
flour beat up, just as you are ready for it,
and dip the fish, so fry it.[39]

Mrs. Harrison first floured her fish and then dip-

ped it in beaten egg before frying it in oil. Her fried

oysters, however, were dipped in a true batter and rolled

in bread crumbs, in the modern fashion.[40]

The thrifty housewife who fried few meats made full

use of her frying pan in the preparation of other articles

of food. The toasts so important as garnishes and as in-

gredients in made dishes and soups were fried like modern

croutons. Either penny loaves or manchet bread made the

best toasts of this kind. But French toast, too, was served:

To make fried toasts.

    Take a penny-loaf, cut it into slices a
quarter of an inch thick round-ways, toast
them, and then take a pint of cream and three
eggs, half a pint of sack, some nutmeg, and
sweetened to your taste. Steep the toasts in
it for three or four hours, then have ready
some butter hot in a pan, put in the toasts
and fry them brown, lay them in a dish, melt
a little butter, and then mix what is left;

---

39. Glasse, Art of Cookery, p. 118.

40. Harrison, Pocket-book, pp. 39, 42.

if none, put in some wine and sugar, and pour over them. They make a pretty plate or side-dish for supper.[41]

Mrs. Glasse's Spanish fritters were quite similar:

Take the inside of a roll, and slice it in three; then soak it in milk; then pass it through a batter of eggs, fry them in oil; when almost done, repass them in another batter; then let them fry till they are done, draw them off the oil, and lay them in a dish; over every pair of fritters you must throw cinnamon, small coloured sugar plumbs, and clarified sugar.[42]

Deep-fat frying also was practiced, but with discretion--chiefly for fritters, as directed by Mrs. Custis:

To make Fritters.

Take a pinte of very stronge ale, put to it a little sack & warme it in a little scillet, then take 8 youlks of eggs & but 2 whites, beat them very well, then put to them a little flowre & beat them together, then put in your warme ale, you must put noe more flowre to the eggs after the ale is in your batter must be noe thicker then will just hang on the apples, season the batter with the powder of nutmegg, cloves, and mace, then cut your apple into little bits & put them into the batter, then set on the fire a good quantety of tryed suet or hoggs lard, & when it is very hot drop in your apples one by one with your fingers as fast as you can when they are fryde lay them on a cleane cloth put over a cullender, then lay them on trencher plates, & strow on them sugar & cinemon.[43]

---

41. Glasse, Art of Cookery, p. 166.

42. Ibid., pp. 368-369.

43. Custis, Booke of Cookery, No. 98; for other sweet fritters see Harrison, Pocket-book, p. 84.

A variation familiar everywhere today was being made in Virginia as

SPANISH FRITTERS.

Make up a quart of flour, with one egg well beaten, a large spoonful of yeast, and as much milk as will make it a little softer than muffin dough; mix it early in the morning; when well risen, work in two spoonsful of melted butter, make it in balls the size of a walnut, and fry them a light brown in boiling lard--eat them with wine and sugar, or molasses.[44]

Finally, Mrs. Randolph offered a second version:

DOUGH NUTS--A YANKEE CAKE.

Dry half a pound of good brown sugar, pound it and mix it with two pounds of flour, and sift it; add two spoonsful of yeast, and as much new milk as will make it like bread: when well risen, knead in half a pound of butter, make it in cakes the size of a half dollar, and fry them a light brown in boiling lard.[45]

Yet not all fritters were fried in deep fat. Mrs. Glasse often recommended quick frying in relatively little butter,[46] as did Mrs. Custis, for her French fritters:

Take a pinte of flowre & add thereto some cheese curd broaken small, & 6 eggs beaten, & about the biggness of an egg in marrow shread small mix these well with halfe a pinte of white wine & some sugar, & a little salt, & add to these some apples shread, & preserv'd

---

44. Randolph, _Virginia Housewife_, p. 130.

45. _Ibid._, p. 133.

46. Glasse, _Art of Cookery_, pp. 156-159. Note that the word _sauté_ was not used commonly in England until the nineteenth century, though directions may specify shaking the pan.

leamon pill & other suckets, then melt some
fresh butter in a frying pan, & fry them in
little lumps about the biggness of a wallnut
or less, & strow on them when they are serv'd
up some sugar, & cinnamon if you please.[47]

All these fritters were sweet, suitable for the sec-

ond course or for supper. Customary batter ingredients

were: eggs or ale for leavening; milk, cream, sack, or

brandy; flour, rice or fine crumbs; seasonings of sugar and

spices, crushed almonds, lemon peel. The most appetizing

solids were currants, chopped apples and other fruits. A

number of oddities, however, were popular--vine leaves, spin-

ach, orange flowers, saffron, parsnips, carrots, skirrets,

and perfumes like ambergris and musk. Fanciful shapes could

be achieved with Mrs. Glasse's syringed fritters:

> Take about a pint of water, and a bit of
> butter the bigness of an egg, with some lemon-
> peel, green if you can get it, rasped preserved
> lemon-peel, and crisped orange-flowers; put all
> together in a stew-pan over the fire, and when
> boiling throw in some fine flour; keep it stir-
> ing, put in by degrees more flour till your
> batter be thick enough, take it off the fire,
> then take an ounce of sweet almonds, four bit-
> ter ones, pound them in a mortar, stir in two
> Naples biscuits crumbled, two eggs beat; stir
> all together, and more eggs, till your batter
> be thin enough to be syringed. Fill your sy-
> ringe, your butter being hot, syringe your
> fritters in it, to make it of a true lovers-
> knot, and being well coloured, serve them up
> for a side-dish.
>   At another time, you may rub a sheet of
> paper with butter, over which you may syringe

---

47. Custis, Booke of Cookery, No. 202.

your fritters, and make them in what shape
your please. Your butter being hot, turn the
paper up-side-down over it, and your fritters
will easily drop off. When fry'd strew them
with sugar, and glaze them.[48]

Another elaborate fritter was made of paste, in-

stead of batter, which could be shaped with the hands

into rolls and other designs or rolled out like regular

pastry and cut into any desired shapes. Fried a "fine

brown," these fritters were useful as garnishes for other

dishes, or they could be served alone.[49]

For similar uses there were miniature fried pies

called pasties or <u>petits</u> <u>patés</u>; for example, Mrs. Smith's

Apple Pasties to fry.

Pare and quarter Apples, and boil them
in Sugar and Water, and a Stick of Cinnamon,
and when tender, put in a little White wine,
the Juice of a Lemon, a Piece of fresh Butter,
and a little Ambergrease or Orange-flower
Water; stir all together, and when 'tis cold,
put it in Puff-paste, and fry them.[50]

"Any fruit you please" could be substituted for the apples,

and chopped pieces of meat or fowl, fish or seafood highly

seasoned offered variety to the "petit pasties for garnish-

ing of dishes."[51]

---

48. Glasse, <u>Art of Cookery</u>, p. 158.

49. <u>Ibid</u>., white fritters, p. 157, and water
fritters, p. 158.

50. Smith, <u>Compleat Housewife</u>, p. 57.

51. Glasse, <u>Art of Cookery</u>, p. 117.

A special French pasty of this sort, a _rissole_, was usually fried in the eighteenth century and used exactly like a petit pasty.[52] Mrs. Bradley's "Rosolis of Marrow" were a mixture of minced apple, marrow, boiled egg yolks and lemon peel held together with cream and seasoned with nutmeg, salt, pepper and sugar and enclosed in paste in this manner:

> When this [the paste] is made roll it thin-
> ner than for Tarts, then cut it into square
> Pieces of the Bigness of Cards, and lay upon
> each of them a Lump of the mixed ingredients
> as large as will conveniently lie upon them to
> be covered in; a small Spoonful is about the
> proper Quantity for each.
> Turn over the thin Crust upon the Ingredi-
> ents, and make the Edges fast in Shape of a
> little Pasty or a Half Moon, close it very well,
> otherwise it will be liable to open in the
> Dressing, and finish the Rosolis by cutting off
> the Edges of the Paste with a Jagg or Runner.[53]

Then they were fried "in Butter clarified, in the Manner of Fritters." Or they might be baked: "They are as well one Way as another, and therefore the judicious House-keeper will consider the Rest of her Table, and chuse either Method accordingly."[54]

---

52. For a French recipe and a summary of its vari-ations from the thirteenth century to modern times, see Prosper Montagné, _Larousse Gastronomique: The Encyclo-pedia of Food, Wine & Cookery_, ed. by Charlotte Turgeon and Nina Froud (New York, 1961), p. 812.

53. Bradley, _British Housewife_, pp. 669-670.

54. For the puff paste commonly used for pasties

Fritter batter was used for another popular fried food, pancakes; these too were usually sweet enough to be served with the dessert course--Mrs. Custis's, for example:

> Take a quart of ale & warme, then mingle
> with it 4 or 5 eggs well beaten, a little flower
> a nutmegg grated, a little rosewater a quarter
> of a pinte of sack & a little salt, mingle all
> these well together, then fry the pancakes very
> thin with fresh butter & serve them up with cin-
> namon & sugar strowed on them.[55]

Mrs. Glasse provided a basic recipe:

To make pancakes.

> Take a quart of milk, beat in six or eight
> eggs, leaving half the whites out; mix it well
> till your batter is of a fine thickness. You
> must observe to mix your flour first with a
> little milk, then add the rest by degrees; put
> in two spoonfuls of beaten ginger, a glasse of
> brandy, a little salt; stir all together, make
> your stew-pan very clean, put in a piece of but-
> ter as big as a walnut, then pour in a ladleful
> of batter, which will make a pancake, moving
> the pan round that the batter be all over the
> pan; shake the pan, and when you think that
> side is enough, toss it; if you can't, turn it
> cleverly, and when both sides are done, lay it
> in a dish before the fire, and so do the rest.
> You must take care they are dry; when you send
> them on table, strew a little sugar over them.[56]

And Mrs. Bradley explained how to follow the recommended procedure with flair:

---

and rissoles, see below pp. 121-122 and for baked pasties, pp. 123-126.

55. Custis, Booke of Cookery, No. 97.

56. Glasse, <u>Art of Cookery</u>, pp. 159-160.

The Art of tossing a Pancake.

This is a Thing very easy to a bold Hand, but which a timerous Person will never be able to do well; for such a one, she is to know that the first Thing to be done is to get rid of her Fear, and then a little Practice will make it quite familiar.

The best Way to learn it is this:

Let a Kitchen Table Cloth be spread upon the Ground at a small Distance from the Fire, and when the first Pancake is ready for turning let the Cook try to toss it over the Cloth; if it falls in right it is very well, and if not there is no Harm done, it will be catched clean, and may do for the Servants Table.

When there is not the Danger of throwing them into the Fire the Cook will have less Fear, and as we have said before, the less Fear the more Likelihood of Success.

The Way is to hold the Pan very steady, and toss the Pancake with a sudden Jerk.

Practice is all; for as the Children play at Bilbecket till they can catch the Ball every Time for many Minutes together, in the same Manner the Cook will be able to toss a hundred Pancakes without missing once, when she is accustomed to the Method of it.[57]

For elegance the pancake had to be very thin. A popular recipe was called a Quire of Paper Pancakes because "when laid one over another they have the Resemblance of a Quire of Paper."[58] This batter was made of rich cream, sack, melted butter, powdered sugar, nutmeg, more eggs than usual, and only a few spoonfuls of flour. A paper pancake was done as soon as it was "just coloured," and instead of

---

57. Bradley, British Housewife, p. 571.

58. Ibid., p. 572; for similar recipes see Glasse, Art of Cookery, p. 160, and Randolph, Virginia Housewife, p. 123.

turning it the cook might take it up and lay it carefully in the warm serving dish with sugar sprinkled over it. Thus separated, the pancakes could be stacked and finally sent to the table as a "quire."

Another conventional dish prepared in a frying pan--the omelet--Dr. Johnson defined as "a kind of pancake made with eggs." Our eighteenth-century English cookbooks contain no recipe for a plain omelet, since every competent cook knew how to make it, but all of them suggested variations in the ingredients added to the beaten eggs. Herbs were used freely, as were chopped vegetables--asparagus, broccoli, spinach, lettuce, green beans, artichoke bottoms, green peas, mushrooms, truffles, morels.[59] Seville oranges were a favorite garnish.

Mrs. Randolph, on the other hand, assumed that un-trained Virginia cooks would profit from instruction in the basic art:

TO MAKE AN OMELETTE.

Break six or eight eggs in a dish, beat them a little, add parsley and chives chopped small, with pepper and salt; mix all well to-gether, put a piece of butter in a pan, let it melt over a clear fire till nearly brown; pour in the eggs, stir it in, and in a few minutes it will be done sufficiently; double it, and dish it quite hot.[60]

---

59. The additions of cheese, chopped ham, fish, seafood, etc. are later conventions.

60. Randolph, <u>Virginia Housewife</u>, p. 88.

Plain scrambled eggs, like an omelet, were not difficult or elegant enough for inclusion in a cookbook. Mrs. Glasse called the process "buttering" eggs; she described it and suggested its use in her recipe for a broccoli and egg dish:

> Boil your brockely tender, saving a large bunch for the middle, and six or eight little thick sprigs to stick round. Take a toast half an inch thick, toast it brown, as big as you would have it for your dish or butter-plate, butter some eggs thus: take six eggs, more or less as you have occasion, beat them well, put them into a sauce-pan with a good piece of butter, a little salt, keep beating them with a spoon till they are thick enough, then pour them on the toast; set the biggest bunch of brockely in the middle, and the other little pieces round and about, and garnish the dish round with little sprigs of brockely. This is a pretty side-dish, or a corner-plate.[61]

The attitude toward fried eggs was similar. While they might be used on top of spinach, asparagus, or another green vegetable, poached or boiled eggs were preferred. For something unusual Mrs. Glasse suggested:

> To fry eggs as round as balls.
>
> Having a deep frying-pan, and three pints of clarified butter, heat it as hot as for fritters, and stir it with a stick, till it runs round like a whirlpool; then break an egg into the middle, and turn it round with your stick, till it be as hard as a poached egg; the whirling round of the butter will make it as round as a ball, then take it up with a slice, and put it in a dish before the

---

61. Glasse, Art of Cookery, p. 192; cf. Custis, Booke of Cookery, No. 44.

fire: they will keep hot half an hour and yet be soft; so you may do as many as you please. You may serve these with what you please, nothing better than stewed spinach, and garnish with orange.[62]

Fried vegetables were all but unknown. Even fried potatoes were a sweet dish until Mrs. Randolph's day. The following recipes illustrate first the convention, then the Virginia adaptation:

To fry potatoes.

Cut them into thin slices, as big as a crown piece, fry them brown, lay them in a plate or dish, pour melted butter, and sack and sugar over them. These are a pretty corner-plate.[63]

TO FRY SLICED POTATOS.

Peel large potatos, slice them about a quarter of an inch thick, or cut them in shavings round and round, as you would peel a lemon; dry them well in a clean cloth, and fry them in lard or dripping. Take care that your fat and frying-pan are quite clean; put it on a quick fire, watch it, and as soon as the lard boils and is still, put in the slices of potatos, and keep moving them till they are crisp; take them up, and lay them to drain on a sieve; send them up with very little salt sprinkled on them.[64]

Mrs. Randolph prepared still another modern favorite, which was then a novelty:

---

62. *Ibid.*, p. 201.

63. *Ibid.*, p. 193.

64. Randolph, *Virginia Housewife*, p. 97.

EGG PLANT.

The purple ones are best; get them young
and fresh; pull out the stem, and parboil them
to take off the bitter taste; cut them in
slices an inch thick, but do not peel them;
dip them in the yelk of an egg, and cover
them with grated bread, a little salt and
pepper--when this has dried, cover the other
side the same way--fry them a nice brown.
They are very delicious, tasting much like
soft crabs....[65]

Though she gave us the earliest version of the old standby

of the rural South--black-eyed peas fried with bacon[66]--

her printed repertoire did not include fried apples or

fried ham with red-eye gravy.

---

65. Ibid., p. 108.

66. This recipe is quoted above p. 67.

V. COOKING METHODS: BAKING

The home brick oven--whether adjacent to the hearth

in the kitchen or a separate structure outside--was de-

signed and used exclusively for bread, cake and pastry.[1]

If the niceties of regulating several fires on the

hearth at one time challenged the skill of the cook, even

more difficult was the proper regulation of the oven.[2]

One built a fire directly in it for the purpose of heat-

ing the walls, which had to hold enough heat long enough

to complete that particular baking load. Since the oven

had no flue, the fire smothered if the door was closed;

therefore, the door was left partly open to supply oxygen

for the fire and to allow the smoke to escape. The open

door also allowed the cook to watch her fire. For even

---

1. When eighteenth-century cookbooks include very
large meat pies and large joints of meat baked in pastry
"coffins," they instruct the cook about sending them to
the oven of a commercial baker. In Virginia towns, as in
rural England and Scotland, such shops were so rare that
this study is restricted to home baking. Cf. Francis W.
Steer, Farm and Cottage Inventories of Mid-Essex, 1635-
1749 (Chelmsford, 1950), p. 27, and Marjorie Plant, The
Domestic Life of Scotland in the Eighteenth Century (Ed-
inburgh, 1952), pp. 77-78.

2. The amount of fuel and the baking time depended
upon the nature of the baking load. Pies and cakes required a hotter oven than bread but shorter baking time.

heat she stirred it periodically and pushed it about to

different spots on the oven floor. When the fuel had

burned to ashy coals, she raked them out and then tested

the heat with her hand. If the oven was too hot, she al-

lowed it to cool to the proper temperature; if it was not

hot enough, she had to repeat the heating procedure with

another fire. Using an oven peel to protect her hands,

she then put in the bread, which had been kneaded earlier

and set to rise so as to be ready to bake when the oven

was ready, and closed the door, not to open it again until

she judged the bread to be done. Small loaves could be

baked directly on the bricks without scorching the bottom

crusts. Large loaves or a very hot oven floor dictated

the use of bread pans, as did cakes and pies of all sorts.

Mrs. Custis's recipe for manchet loaves included

useful directions for managing the oven:

> To make white bread.
>
> Take 3 quarters of a peck of fine flower &
> strow salt in as much as will season it, then
> heat as much milke as will season it luke warme,
> & hould it high when you poure it on to make
> it light, & mingle with your milke 4 or 5 spoon-
> fulls of good yeast, worke your paste well, &
> then let it ly a rising by the fire, your oven
> will be heated in an houre & halfe then shut
> it up a quarter of an houre, in which space
> make up your loaves & then set them in the oven,
> an houre & halfe will bake them.[3]

---

3. Frances Parke Custis, A Booke of Cookery, No.
95. This kind of bread was the manchet loaf made by

As with country housewives in our own time, the mat-
ter of keeping on hand a supply of "good yeast" required
good management. The preferred kind was barm, the froth
that forms on the top of fermenting ale or beer. The ale
itself could be used, as in Mrs. Custis's recipe for a
sweet bread similar to the popular cheese loaf:

> To make A butterd loafe.
>
> Take 4 quarts of milke put runnit to it &
> whey it & hang the curd up in a cloth to dreyne
> for an houre or 2, then take 10 eggs & leave
> out 3 of the whites then take a little ginger,
> a pinte of ale yeast, as much fine flowre as
> will make it up to a loafe. when it is well
> baked cut it up, & butter it with sweete but-
> ter & sugar your butter must be melted & beat
> up with the sugar before your put it into
> your loafe.[4]

Mrs. Glasse suggested a way to dry yeast for future

use:

> When you have yeast in plenty, take a quan-
> tity of it, stir and work it well with a wisk
> until it becomes liquid and thin, then get a
> large wooden platter, cooler, or tub, clean
> and dry, and with a soft brush, lay a thin lay-
> er of the yeast on the tub, and turn the mouth
> downwards that no dust may fall upon it, but so
> that the air may get under to dry it. When
> that coat is very dry, then lay on another coat
> and let it dry, and so go on to put one coat
> upon another till you have a sufficient quan-
> tity, even two or three inches thick, to serve
> for several months, always taking care the
> yeast in the tub be very dry before you lay

---

commercial bakers; cf. [Hannah Glasse], "To make white
bread, after the London way," The Art of Cookery... (7th
edn., London, 1760), p. 297.

4. Ibid., No. 93.

more on. When you have occasion to make use
of this yeast cut a piece off, and lay it in
warm water; stir it together, and it will be
fit for use.[5]

And an alternative way to preserve one's leaven for a

shorter time:

> Take a lump of dough, about two pounds of
> your last making, which has been raised by barm,
> keep it by you in a wooden vessel, and cover it
> well with flour. This is your leaven; then the
> night before you intend to bake, put the said
> leaven to a peck of flour, and work them well
> together with warm water. Let it lye in a dry
> wooden vessel, well covered with a linen cloth
> and a blanket, and keep it in a warm place.
> This dough kept warm will rise again next morn-
> ing, and will be sufficient to mix with two or
> three bushels of flour, being worked up with
> warm water and a little salt. [Then proceed
> as usual.][6]

With the proper care, the tough crustiness of French

bread could be produced at home:

> Take three quarts of water, and one of
> milk; in winter scalding hot, in summer a lit-
> tle more than milk-warm. Season it well with
> salt, then take a pint and a half of good ale
> yeast not bitter, lay it in a gallon of water
> the night before, pour it off the water, stir
> in your yeast into the milk and water, then
> with your hand break in a little more than a
> quarter of a pound of butter, work it well till
> it is dissolved, then beat up two eggs in a ba-
> son, and stir them in, have about a peck and a
> half of flour, mix it with your liquor; in

---

5. Glasse, Art of Cookery, pp. 299-300; cf. the
"PATENT YEAST" suggested for country housewives in Mary
Randolph, The Virginia Housewife... (Philadelphia, 1855),
pp. 137-138.

6. Ibid., p. 299.

winter make your dough pretty stiff, in summer
more slack; so that you may use a little more
or less of flour, according to the stiffness
of your dough; mix it well, but the less you
work it the better. Make it into rolls, and
have a very quick oven, but not to burn. When
they have lain about a quarter of an hour turn
them on the other side, let them lie about a
quarter longer, take them out and chip all your
French bread with a knife, which is better than
rasping it, and makes it look spungy and of a
fine yellow, whereas the rasping takes of all
that fine colour, and makes it look too smooth.
You must stir your liquor into the flour as
your do for pye-crust. After your dough is
made cover it with a cloth, and let it lie to
rise while the oven is heating.[7]

Mrs. Custis detailed the discriminating use of the combi-

nation of oven peel and woolen cloths:

To make French Bread.

Take a gallon of flowre & put to it a little salt, a pinte of ale yeast, a quart of new
milke heated, but not too hot, poure these into the flowre, & mix them with one hand you
must not knead it at all, then heat a woollen
cloth & poure your paste on it, flower the
cloth, & lap it up, then make it into a dosin
of loves & set them on a peele flowred, & lay
a warm wollen cloth on them, your oven must be
allmoste hot when you mix your bread heat your
oven pritty hot, & chip your bread when it
comes out.[8]

While loaf bread was leavened only with yeast, small

rolls or buns contained eggs as well, and sometimes sugar

and spice. Mrs. Smith's plain buns were standard:

---

7. Ibid., pp. 297-298.

8. Custis, Booke of Cookery, No. 92.

Take two Pounds of fine Flour, a Pint of
Ale-yeast; put a little Sack in the Yeast, and
three Eggs beaten; knead all these together
with a little warm Milk, a little Nutmeg, and
a little Salt; then lay it before the Fire till
it rise very light; then knead in a Pound of
fresh Butter, and a Pound of round Carraway-
comfits; and bake them in a quick Oven, on
floured Papers, in what Shape you please.[9]

In Dr. Johnson's London it was fashionable to eat a

special bun with one's breakfast tea on Good Friday--a

cross-bun, made from any soft dough suitable for a small

roll, then scored twice across the top so that it would

come out of the oven with an indentation depicting a

cross.[10] For Lenten fare there were wigs, which were

made from a special dough cut into wedges; Pepys ate

these with ale,[11] the customary beverage in the seven-

teenth century. Of Mrs. Smith's five recipes for wigs,

the following gave explicit baking instructions:

Take three Pounds and a half of Flour, and
three quarters of a Pound of Butter, and rub
it into the Flour till none of it be seen; then
take a Pint or more of new Milk, and make it
very warm, and half a Pint of new Ale-yeast;
then make it into a light Paste. Put in Carra-
way-seeds, and what Spice you please; then make

---

9. E. Smith, The Compleat Housewife... (Williamsburg, 1742), p. 75; Mrs. Glasse copied it exactly, Art of
Cookery, p. 277.

10. Hot cross-buns were cried in the streets by
vendors.

11. Samuel Pepys, Diary and Correspondence..., ed.
by Richard, Lord Braybrooke (4 vols., London, 1889-1897),
II, 41, entry of April 8, 1664.

it up, and lay it before the Fire to rise; then
work in three quarters of a Pound of Sugar, and
then roll them into what Form you please pretty
thin, and put them on Tin-plates, and hold them
before the Oven to rise again. Before you set
them in, your Oven must be pretty quick.[12]

The year round, gingerbread occupied a special place
in taste and tradition. Though crisp, sweet, and spicy,
it was a true bread, well known in Shakespeare's day.
Properly made it would stay crisp in damp weather and remain edible for years.[13] In tradition it was associated
with fairs, and a gingerbread man had long been a favorite
"fairing." The gingerbread booth, always the most colorful booth at the fair, was decorated with elaborate fig-
ures--kings, queens, coronets, animals, birds--shaped in
special gingerbread molds and then ornamented with sheets
or strips of gold leaf.[14] By the time the gilded figures
were in place amidst gaily colored streamers and bright
ribbon bows, the booth dazzled the eyes of the children
and their unsophisticated elders. Apparently the gilt
figures were never eaten, though they were for sale along

---

12. Smith, Compleat Housewife, p. 76; for other
recipes see pp. 65, 67, 74, 79. Mrs. Glasse, Art of
Cookery, pp. 277, 355, has three recipes.

13. John Ashton, The History of Bread... (London,
1904), p. 152.

14. Sometimes an alloy was used--Dutch metal, e.g.,
a combination of zinc and copper.

with the less elaborate gingerbread nuts[15] and molded figures.

All cookbooks contained gingerbread recipes: Mrs.
Smith had five, Mrs. Bradley five, Mrs. Custis five, Mrs.
Glasse two, Mrs. Harrison two, Mrs. Randolph three. Though
the ingredients varied widely, the finished product was hard
and crisp, sweet and spicy and resistant to moisture. Ginger and butter were standard. The sweetening agent might
be honey, treacle, or sugar; the leavening, either ale yeast
or potash. If more liquid was needed, cream, sack, claret,
or vinegar might be used. Earlier recipes called for bread
crumbs, as in boiled puddings; later ones suggested flour.
Special additions included other spices--nutmeg, cinnamon,
cloves or mace--and the almonds, raisins, dates, orange
peel or lemon peel so popular in puddings. The finished
dough was either shaped by hand, printed by being pressed
into a mold, or rolled out in a sheet and cut into the
desired shapes.

Sometimes the leavening was omitted, as in Mrs.
Glasse's gingerbread cakes:

> Take three pounds of flour, one pound of
> sugar, one pound of butter rubbed in very fine,
> two ounces of ginger beat fine, a large nutmeg
> grated; then take a pound of treacle, a quarter

---

15. The most famous gingerbread vendor, Tiddy Ford,
appears in Hogarth's drawing with gingerbread nuts in his
basket; for a sketch of the drawing see Ashton, History
of Bread, p. 154.

of a pint of cream, make them warm together,
and make up the bread stiff; roll it out, and
make it up into thin cakes, cut them out with
a tea-cup, or small glass, or roll them round
like nuts, and bake them on tin plates in a
slack oven.[16]

For greater ease in printing an elaborate shape, a special

gelatinous substance was sometimes added, as in Mrs. Cus-

tis's white gingerbread:

Take halfe a pound of blanched allmonds 2
ounces of cinnamon, & put in ginger to your
taste, a pound of searced sugar, A penny loafe
grated of white bread & dry it & searce it
over night, & put some gum dragon to steep in
rose water, then beat your almonds in a morter
& now and then put in a spoonfull of your
spices sugar & crums of bread and sometimes
sprinkle in a little sack, and toward the lat-
ter end of your beating, put in some of your
gum to binde all together, and when it is well
beat & mixed in the morter, you may make it
into roles or print it according to your plea-
sure, but it is best to roule it out & print it,
the prints of white ginger bread are used much
thinner then the cullerd, which is commonly
made allmoste halfe an Intch thick or a quarter of an intch at the least.[17]

Another popular sweet bread was the biscuit now

called a cooky in America, and biscuits were known in many

variations on the basic recipe:

To make common biscuits.

Beat up six eggs, with a spoonful of rose
water and a spoonful of sack, then add a pound
of fine powdered sugar, and a pound of flour;
mix them into the eggs by degrees, and an ounce

---

16. Glasse, Art of Cookery, p. 273.

17. Custis, A Booke of Sweetmeats, No. 189.

of coriander-seeds, mix all well together,
shape them on white thin paper, or tin moulds,
in any form you please. Beat the white of an
egg, with a feather rub them over, and dust
fine sugar over them. Set them in an oven
moderately heated, till they rise and come to
a good colour, take them out; and when you
have done with the oven, if you have no stove
to dry them in, put them in the oven again,
and let them stand all night to dry.[18]

In addition to the paper and tin molds recommended, tin

sheets and shallow tin plates were suitable for baking

biscuits. Mrs. Glasse used cooky sheets for her drop

biscuits, a thinner dough beaten very light and dropped

by spoonfuls on the greased tin sheets.[19] For macaroons

she recommended the combination of paper and tin plates:

Take a pound of almonds, let them be
scalded, blanched, and thrown into cold water,
then dry them in a cloth, and pound them in
a mortar, moisten them with orange-flower
water, or the white of an egg, lest they turn
to oil; afterwards take an equal quantity of
fine powder sugar, with three or four whites
of eggs, and a little musk, beat all well together, and shape them on wafer-paper with a
spoon round. Bake them in a gentle oven on
tin plates.[20]

Another favorite, similar to a macaroon, was the

ratafia biscuit, which was made with bitter almonds:

---

18. Glasse, Art of Cookery, pp. 275-276.

19. Ibid., p. 275.

20. Ibid., p. 276. See also Custis, Booke of
Sweetmeats, No. 184; Smith Compleat Housewife, p. 77;
and for Jefferson's Paris recipe, Marie Kimball, Thomas
Jefferson's Cook Book (Richmond, 1949), p. 37.

Take four Ounces of bitter Almonds, blanch
and beat them as fine as you can; in beating
them, put in the Whites of four Eggs, one at a
Time; then mix it up with sifted Sugar to a
light Paste; roll them, and lay them on Wafer
Paper, and on Tin plates; make the Paste so
light that you may take it up with a Spoon.
Bake them in a quick Oven.[21]

Shrewsbury cakes were thinner and crisper:

Take to one Pound of Sugar, three Pounds
of the finest Flour, a Nutmeg grated, some
beaten Cinamon; the Sugar and Spice must be
sifted into the Flour, and wet it with three
Eggs, and as much melted Butter as will make
it of a good Thickness to roll into a Paste;
mould it well and roll it, and cut it into
what Shape you please. Perfume them, and
prick them before they go into the Oven.[22]

Jumbals were made of a firm dough that could be

shaped in the hands or cut into fancy shapes:

Take a pound of fine flour and a pound of
fine powder-sugar, make them into light paste,
with whites of eggs beat fine; then add half
a pint of cream, half a pound of fresh butter
melted, and a pound of blanched almonds well
beat. Kneed them all together thoroughly,
with a little rose-water, and cut out your
jumballs in what figures you fancy; and either
bake them in a gentle oven, or fry them in
fresh butter, and they make a pretty side or
corner dish. You may melt a little butter
with a spoonful of sack, and throw fine sugar
all over the dish. If you make them in pretty

---

21. Smith, Compleat Housewife, p. 95. Elizabeth
Raffald, The Experienced English House-keeper... (4th
edn., London, 1775), p. 269, uses half bitter almonds
and half sweet.

22. Ibid., p. 77; cf. Glasse, Art of Cookery, p.
276, without spices, and Randolph, Virginia Housewife,
p. 135, with brandy and coriander seeds added.

figures, they make a fine little dish.[23]

The Savoy and Naples biscuits often used in dessert puddings[24] were similar to modern ladyfingers; they could be purchased commercially packed in tins, but they could also be made at home, as directed by Mrs. Randolph:

SAVOY OR SPUNGE CAKE.

Take twelve fresh eggs, put them in the scale, and balance them with sugar: take out half, and balance the other half with flour; separate the whites from the yelks, whip them up very light, then mix them, and sift in, first sugar, then flour, till both are exhausted; add some grated lemon peel; bake them in paper cases, or little tin moulds. This also makes an excellent pudding, with butter, sugar, and wine, for sauce.[25]

NAPLES BISCUIT.

Beat twelve eggs light, add to them one pound of flour, and one of powdered sugar; continue to beat all together till perfectly light; bake it in long pans, four inches wide, with divisions; so that each cake, when done, will be four inches long, and one and a half wide.[26]

Thinner and crisper than biscuits were the wafers which were baked in the oven or in wafer irons. Mrs. Glasse suggested two simple batters for the oven:

---

23. Glasse, Art of Cookery, pp. 109-110; see also Custis, Booke of Sweetmeats, No. 191-194. Other flavorings included perfume, lemon, caraway seeds, barberries.

24. See trifle and similar made dishes.

25. Randolph, Virginia Housewife, p. 134; cf. Jefferson's Paris recipe, Jefferson's Cook Book, pp. 36-37.

26. Ibid., p. 135.

To make white wafers.

Beat the yolk of an egg and mix it with
a quarter of a pint of fair water; then mix
half a pound of best flour, and thin it with
damask rose-water till you think it of a
proper thickness to bake. Sweeten it to your
palate with fine sugar finely sifted.

To make brown wafers.

Take a quart of ordinary cream, then take
the yolks of three or four eggs, and as much
fine flour as will make it into a thin batter;
sweeten it with three quarters of a pound of
fine sugar finely searsed, and as much pounded
cinnamon as will make it taste. Do not mix
them till the cream be cold; butter your pans,
and make them very hot before you bake them.[27]

As one would expect, it was only the American, Mrs.
Randolph, who baked corn bread of any kind. Her batter
bread mixed flour and corn meal:

Take six spoonsful of flour and three of
corn meal, with a little salt--sift them, and
make a thin batter with four eggs, and a sufficient quantity of rich milk; bake it in little tin moulds in a quick oven.[28]

She made corn meal bread without flour:

Rub a piece of butter the size of an egg,
into a pint of corn meal--make it a batter

---

27. Glasse, Art of Cookery, p. 347; her other wafers are confections of fruit jelly spread on glass sheets
and dried. For similar recipes, but baked in wafer irons,
see Custis, Booke of Sweetmeats, No. 143, and Randolph,
Virginia Housewife, p. 142. Wafer irons, originally designed for making sacramental bread, would accommodate any
thin batter and so were used for secular purposes; the
waffle iron common in the nineteenth century was larger
and usually rectangular in shape.

28. Randolph, Virginia Housewife, p. 140.

with two eggs, and some new milk--add a spoonful of yeast, set it by the fire an hour to
rise, butter little pans, and bake it.[29]

Her mixed bread contained corn meal gruel:

> Put a tea-spoonful of salt, and a large
> one of yeast, into a quart of flour; make it
> sufficiently soft, with corn meal gruel; when
> well risen, bake it in a mould. It is an ex-
> cellent bread for breakfast. Indifferent
> flour will rise much better, when made with
> gruel than with fair water.[30]

Another native product was an important ingredient

in a bread which Mrs. Randolph called:

SWEET POTATO BUNS.

> Boil and mash a potato, rub into it as
> much flour as will make it like bread--add
> spice and sugar to your taste, with a spoon-
> ful of yeast; when it has risen well, work
> in a piece of butter, bake it in small rolls,
> to be eaten hot with butter, either for
> breakfast or tea.[31]

Finally, her hot biscuits were a forerunner of the

Southern specialty, but they were leavened with yeast:

TO MAKE NICE BISCUIT.

> Rub a large spoonful of butter into a
> quart of risen dough, knead it well, and
> make it into biscuit, either thick or thin:
> bake them quickly.[32]

Large cakes were similar to modern pound cake in

---

29. _Ibid._, p. 141.

30. _Ibid._, p. 137; cf. modern salt-rising bread.

31. _Ibid._, p. 141.

32. _Ibid._, p. 137.

texture but with the addition of spices and chopped fruit.

The leavening agent was either ale yeast or eggs or both.

Mrs. Raffald offered general directions for cake making:

Observations upon CAKES.

When you make any kinds of cakes, be sure
that you get the things ready before you begin,
then beat your eggs well, and don't leave them
till you have finished the cakes, or else they
will go back again, and your cakes will not be
light; if your cakes are to have butter in,
take care you beat it to a fine cream before
you put in your sugar, for if you beat it twice
the time, it will not answer so well: as to
plum-cake, seed-cake, or rice-cake, it is best
to bake them in wood garths, for if you bake
them in either pot or tin, they burn the outside of the cakes, and confine them so that the
heat cannot penetrate into the middle of your
cake, and prevents it from rising: bake all
kinds of cake in a good oven, according to the
size of your cake, and follow the directions of
your receipt, for though care hath been taken
to weigh and measure every article belonging to
every kind of cake, yet the management and the
oven must be left to the maker's care.[33]

Mrs. Glasse's pound cake was made of a pound each

of butter, sugar and flour; a dozen egg yolks and half a

dozen whites; caraway seeds or a pound of currants for

seasoning. Mixing it required an hour of beating, and

baking it, another hour in a quick oven.[34]

Mrs. Smith's white cake was a thinner batter made

---

33. Raffald, English House-keeper, p. 264.

34. Glasse, Art of Cookery, p. 272. Mrs. Randolph's
"POUND CAKE," Virginia Housewife, pp. 133-134, is similar
but she suggests that the same batter makes an excellent
pudding, either baked or boiled, and served with wine sauce.

from three quarts of flour, five ounces of sugar, a pound
and a half of butter, nine egg whites and five yolks, half
a pint of ale yeast, a pint of cream, and flavoring of mace,
rose water, sack and currants; it was baked an hour and a
half in a tin hoop.[35] Her rich great cake required a peck
of flour, four pounds of butter, a pound and a half of sugar, twenty egg yolks, three pints of ale yeast, five pints
of cream, a pint of sack; it was flavored with nutmeg,
cloves, mace, cinnamon, orange flower water, musk, ambergris, thirteen pounds or currants, three of raisins, two
of citron, and one of candied lemon peel; and it was baked
four hours in a quick oven.[36] This was the conventional
wedding cake.

Mrs. Raffald's version, called Bride Cake, required
four pounds of flour, four of butter, two of sugar, thirty-
two eggs, half a pint of brandy; mace and nutmeg; chopped
fruit and nuts for additional flavor and body--four pounds
of currants, one each of almonds, citron, and candied orange and lemon peel; it was baked three hours covered with
paper and then iced with a mixture of egg whites, sugar
and almond paste.[37]

---

35. Smith, Compleat Housewife, p. 80.

36. Ibid., pp. 69-70.

37. Raffald, English House-keeper, pp. 264-266.

For seed cakes the popular preference was caraway.
A very rich one called Nun's Cake, favored by Mrs. Smith
and Mrs. Glasse, required four pounds each of flour and
butter, three pounds of sugar, thirty-five egg yolks and
twenty whites, six ounces of caraway seeds, and either
rose water, orange flower water or ambergris; it was baked
three hours in a moderate oven.[38] The category was extensive, however, and variations in the recipes permitted
economy in size, in baking time, and in the use of the
more expensive ingredients. Mrs. Smith, for example, offered six other recipes in which ale yeast or cream was
substituted for part of the eggs and for perfume, either
sack or spices.[39]

Ingredients of the traditional fruit cake were suggested in several combinations. Mrs. Smith's four recipes
were all similar to her rich great cake.[40] In Mrs. Harrison's "Plumb Cake" currants might be supplemented with
"what Sweetmeats you will" and her "Fine Cake" specified
citron, orange and lemon peel as well as currants.[41]

---

38. Smith, Compleat Housewife, pp. 83-84; Glasse,
Art of Cookery, pp. 273-274.

39. Smith, Compleat Housewife, pp. 70-71, 78-80, 83.

40. Ibid., pp. 70, 71, 82, 83.

41. Sarah Harrison, The House-keeper's Pocket-book...
(6th edn., London, 1755), p. 73.

Mrs. Glasse apparently preferred plum pudding, for she

included only one plum cake, which contained no fruit ex-

cept currants and was baked in small buns.[42] Mrs. Ran-

dolph, as was her custom, offered specific instructions

for mixing and baking:

A RICH FRUIT CAKE.

Have the following articles prepared, before you begin the cake: four pounds of flour
dried and sifted, four pounds of butter washed
to free it from salt, two pounds of loaf sugar
pounded, a quarter of a pound of mace, the
same of nutmegs powdered; wash four pounds of
currants clean, pick and dry them; blanch one
pound of sweet almonds, and cut them in very
thin slices; stone two pounds of raisins, cut
them in two, and strew a little flour over to
prevent their sticking together, and two pounds
of citron sliced thin; break thirty eggs, sep-
arating the yelks and whites; work the butter
to a cream with your hand--put in alternately,
flour, sugar, and the froth from both whites
and yelks, which must be beaten separately,
and only the froth put in. When all are mixed
and the cake looks very light, add the spice,
with half a pint of brandy, the currants and
almonds; butter the mould well, pour in part
of the cake, strew over it some raisins and
citron--do this until all is in: set it in a
well heated oven; when it has risen, and the
top is coloured, cover it with paper; it will
require three hours baking--it must be iced.[43]

The all-purpose pie crust of the eighteenth century

was puff paste, made with slight variations in ingredients

and mixing method according to size and kind of pie. Mrs.

---

42. Glasse, "To make little plumcakes," Art of
Cookery, p. 278.

43. Randolph, Virginia Housewife, pp. 134-135.
Strangely, Mrs. Custis had no great cake recipes.

Bradley explained that "Paste is of several Kinds according to the various Purposes for which it is wanted; some being light and more tender, others stronger and firmer, some richer and others plainer...."[44]

Mrs. Glasse's basic recipe might well be used today:

Puff-paste.

Take a quarter of a peck of flour, rub
fine half a pound of butter, a little salt,
make it up into a light paste with cold water,
just stiff enough to work it well up; then
roll it out, and stick pieces of butter all
over, and strew a little flour; roll it up,
and roll it out again; and so do nine or ten
times, till you have rolled in a pound and a
half of butter. This crust is mostly used for
all sorts of pies.[45]

A light hand in the mixing--hallmark of the superior pastry cook--was urged by Mrs. Randolph: "...touch it very lightly with the hands in making--bake it in a moderate oven, that will permit it to rise, but will not make it brown. Good paste must look white, and as light as a feather."[46]

The strong, firm paste needed for large meat pies was mixed with egg yolks and shortening melted in hot water; suet might be substituted for part of the butter, and

---

44. Martha Bradley, The British Housewife... (London, [c. 1770]), p. 61.

45. Glasse, Art of Cookery, p. 145; for two similar recipes see Harrison, Pocket-book, pp. 57-58.

46. Randolph, Virginia Housewife, p. 115.

repeated folding and rolling were not required.[47] A wide
range of fillings for these "pastry coffins" was suggested
to supplement the ingenuity of the hostess in the use of
leftovers and to vary the winter fare, which must have
been monotonous at best.

Mrs. Custis copied out more than twenty recipes, both
simple and elaborate, featuring beef, veal, pork, mutton,
venison, rabbit, fowl, fish, and shellfish. Whole fowls
or fish and legs or rumps of large animals were stuffed and
baked in the crust with a gravy seasoned with herbs, spices,
wine, mushrooms, chestnuts, onions, and the like. Sliced
or chopped, any parts of any kind of meat in any combination were considered suitable for meat pies: feet and
heads, tongues, sweetbreads, hearts, livers, inferior cuts
and leftovers. Even the humble pie, originally suitable
only for servants, was now pepped up with spices and wine
and served to guests.[48] Mrs. Custis's most elaborate mixture, called Pasty Royal, was made of chopped leg of mutton, bacon, neat's tongue, sweetbreads, kidneys, roasted
eggs, sausages, oysters, cockles, mushrooms, artichokes,
asparagus, chestnuts, grapes; seasoned with spices, sweet

---

47. Recipes in Bradley, British Housewife, p. 61;
Glasse, Art of Cookery, p. 145; Raffald, English House-
keeper, pp. 145-146.

48. Custis, Booke of Cookery, No. 64.

herbs, garlic, wine vinegar, capers "and other pickles."[49]

Sweet pies, suitable for second-course dishes, required double crusts, which would be filled with fruits-- apples, pears, plums, apricots, quinces, cherries, lemons, oranges--or mincemeat. Puff paste was preferred, but several substitutes were acceptable. Cream and eggs might replace part of the butter to make it "a quicker way,"[50] or the flour and butter might be beaten together instead of rolled and folded.[51] It was this beaten crust that Mrs. Glasse recommended for the tarts considered more elegant for company and certainly easier to serve than large pies:

> To make different sorts of tarts.
>
> If you bake in tin-patties, butter them, and you must put a little crust all over, because of the taking them out; if in china, or glass, no crust but the top one. Lay fine sugar at the bottom, then your plumbs, cherries, or any other sort of fruit, and sugar at top; then put on your lid, and bake them in a slack oven. Mince pies must be baked in tin-patties, because of taking them out, and puff-paste is best for them. All sweet tarts the beaten crust is best; but as you fancy. You have the receipt for the crusts in this chapter. Apple, pear, apricot, &c. make thus: apples and pears, pare them, cut them into quarters, and core them; cut the quarters a-cross again, set them

---

49. _Ibid._, No. 199.

50. _Ibid._, No. 146. Sometimes sugar was added for crispness, as in Raffald, _English House-keeper_, pp. 144-145.

51. Harrison, _Pocket-book_, p. 58; Glasse, _Art of Cookery_, p. 144. For method of mixing, cf. the nineteenth-century beaten biscuit.

on in a sauce-pan with just as much water as
will barely cover them, let them simmer on a
slow fire just till the fruit is tender; put
a good piece of lemon-peel in the water with
the fruit, then have your patties ready. Lay
fine sugar at bottom, then your fruit, and a
little sugar at top; that you must put in at
your discretion. Pour over each tart a teaspoonful of lemon-juice, and three tea-spoon-
fuls of the liquor they were boiled in; put on
your lid, and bake them in a slack oven. Apricots do the same way, only don't use lemon.[52]

All these fruit tarts are still considered attractive

desserts, fit to set before the most discriminating guest.

And eighteenth-century mincemeat recipes have not been im-

proved. Mrs. Custis's, for example, required equal quanti-

ties of leg of veal (or neat's tongue) and beef suet; a

dozen apples to four pounds of meat; raisins, currants,

candied orange and lemon peel, citron, almonds, sugar and

spices, rose water and wine (either sack or muscatel).[53]

Mrs. Glasse used both brandy and sack and added lemon juice

before baking.[54]

When fresh fruits were not available, preserved fruits

and berries were used to make sweetmeat tarts, as follows:

...only lay in your preserved fruit, and
put a very thin crust at top, and let them be
baked as little as possible; but if you would

---

52. Glasse, Art of Cookery, p. 144.

53. Custis, Booke of Cookery, No. 63; cf. Harrison, Pocket-book, pp. 64-65.

54. Glasse, Art of Cookery, pp. 142-143.

make them very nice, have a large patty, the
size you would have your tart. Make your sugar-
crust, roll it as thick as a halfpenny; then
butter your patties, and cover it. Shape your
upper-crust on a hollow thing on purpose, the
size of your patty, and mark it with a marking-
iron for that purpose, in what shape you please,
to be hollow and open to see the fruit through;
then bake your crust in a very slack oven, not
to discolour it, but to have it crisp. When
the crust is cold, very carefully take it out,
and fill it with what fruit you please, lay on
the lid, and it is done; therefore if the tart
is not eat, your sweetmeat is not the worse,
and it looks genteel.[55]

The ingredients used in either meat pies or fruit

tarts were often enclosed in small squares or circles of

paste that could be shaped as desired and baked as petits

patés.[56] The meat pasties were served as side dishes in

the first course or as garnishes; fruit pasties belonged

in the second course, like tarts.

The ever popular puddings that were not boiled were

usually baked in round "coffins" without top crusts, like

modern custard pies and tarts. These were true custards

made of sugar, eggs and cream, with the addition of rai-

sins, almonds, bread crumbs or rice, and flavored in any

of the customary ways. There were also cheesecakes, made

with rennet to curdle the milk and cream, or with lemon

peel and juice instead of rennet and large quantities of

---

55. Ibid., p. 144; cf. Custis, Booke of Cookery,
No. 66-68.

56. See above p. 96.

butter and eggs instead of cream. All these custards

could be baked as puddings in a slow oven, without pastry,

if desired, but for guests a pastry shell was apparently

de rigueur.[57]

Quite in the conventional fashion Mrs. Randolph of-

fered adaptations, using New World products:

BAKED INDIAN MEAL PUDDING.

Boil one quart of milk, mix in it two gills
and a half of corn meal very smoothly, seven
eggs well beaten, a gill of molasses, and a good
piece of butter; bake it two hours.[58]

SWEET POTATO PUDDING.

Boil one pound of sweet potatos very tender, rub them while hot through a colander;
add six eggs well beaten, three quarters of
a pound of powdered sugar, three quarters of
butter, and some grated nutmeg and lemon peel,
with a glass of brandy; put a paste in the
dish, and when the pudding is done, sprinkle
the top with sugar, and cover it with bits of
citron. Irish potato pudding is made in the
same manner, but is not so good.[59]

PUMPKIN PUDDING.

Stew a fine sweet pumpkin till soft and
dry; rub it through a sieve, mix with the pulp
six eggs quite light, a quarter of a pound of
butter, half a pint of new milk, some pounded

---

57. Smith, Compleat Housewife, pp. 54-68; Harrison, Pocket-book, pp. 50-56; Glasse, Art of Cookery, pp. 278-280; Raffald, English House-keeper, pp. 256-260; Custis, Booke of Cookery, No. 74, 77, 82, 104, 106-108.

58. Randolph, Virginia Housewife, p. 126.

59. Ibid., pp. 120-121. Mrs. Glasse also has an Irish potato pudding and pie which validate Mrs. Randolph's opinion. Glasse, Art of Cookery, pp. 206, 244.

ginger and nutmeg, a wine glass of brandy, and
sugar to your taste. Should it be too liquid,
stew it a little drier, put a paste round the
edges, and in the bottom of a shallow dish or
plate--pour in the mixture, cut some thin bits
of paste, twist them, and lay them across the
top, and bake it nicely.[60]

By the end of the century, when ovens were larger

and more readily available in Virginia towns, other foods

were being baked. For this reason, Mrs. Randolph recom-

mended many baked dishes unknown to Mrs. Glasse, though

the ingredients were familiar. Large cuts of beef, lamb,

or mutton, a whole pig, or a large fish were stuffed with

forcemeat and baked in gravy without a pastry coffin. Her

favorite seasonings were salt and pepper, garlic, parsley,

wine; while she occasionally used the conventional mush-

room and walnut catsups, she also introduced ripe tomatoes

into her mutton gravy.[61] Another innovation was a baked

vegetable dish now a standard item in Southern cookery:

TO SCOLLOP TOMATOS.

Peel off the skin from large, full, ripe
tomatos--put a layer in the bottom of a deep
dish, cover it well with bread grated fine;
sprinkle on pepper and salt, and lay some
bits of butter over them--put another layer
of each, till the dish is full--let the top
be covered with crumbs and butter--bake it
a nice brown.[62]

---

60. Ibid., p. 127.

61. Ibid., pp. 29-30, 33, 35-37, 44-47, 52.

62. Ibid., p. 101.

FIREPLACE BAKING

Many Virginia housewives--probably most of them--
having no brick oven, did all their baking on the hearth;
and the more fortunate ones substituted fireplace equipment for the oven in small baking chores.

There were several expedients. The simplest was
to sweep a clean spot on the hearth and place a piece of
dough directly on the hot bricks, cover it with an upside-
down pot of iron or earthenware, then cover the pot with
embers and pile hot coals around it.[63] A special iron
pot called a bake kettle or Dutch oven could be used for
either bread, cakes, pastries, or small cuts of meat. It
stood on short legs and had a flat, tight-fitting lid.
Heat was supplied by a bed of coals beneath the Dutch oven
and hot embers piled on the top and around it.

As in other phases of fireplace cooking, experience
dictated baking time and the cook regulated the heat for
her bake kettle or pot under the same principles that gov-
erned her control of the fires for other utensils. Recipes, therefore, did not usually specify particular baking
equipment; furthermore, they were prepared for housewives
who presumably would buy cookbooks only if they owned

---

63. This method is described in L. A. Shuffrey, The
English Fireplace (London, [1912]), p. 63, and Gertrude
Jekyll, Old English Household Life (London, 1933), p. 51.

extensive cooking equipment and knew how to use it. Mrs. Randolph's recipes, in this particular too, were exceptional; in a number of them she stated a preference for using a Dutch oven--to brown flour for gravy or pieces of meat to be baked in gravy, and to bake small custards or other egg dishes.[64]

A third kind of baking utensil was the round iron griddle, a refinement of the ancient flat baking-stone still used in Scottish cottages for bannocks, scones and oatcakes. Suspended by its handle from a pothook, like a kettle, it was used for baking thin pancakes made from the same kind of batter that was fried in a frying pan and, more often, for thicker cakes of the consistency of dough--principally muffins and crumpets.

Eighteenth-century muffins, like crumpets, were light and spongy, first baked on a griddle and later toasted and buttered for breakfast or tea. To make muffins by Mrs. Glasse's instructions, mix a soft dough or flour, salt and thin ale and let it rise in the mixing trough; then break off pieces of dough and shape them by hand into small balls or disks, cover them with a flannel cloth and allow them to rise a second time. To bake them:

---

64. Randolph, Virginia Housewife, pp. 15, 28, 33, 36, 55, 57, 63, 68, 86, 87, 99, 147.

...lay them on your iron; as one side begins to change colour turn the other, and take
great care they don't burn, or be too much dis-
coloured, but that you will be a judge of in
two or three makings. Take care the middle of
the iron is not too hot, as it will be, but
then you may put a brickbat or two in the middle of the fire to slacken the heat....
    When you eat them, toast them with a fork
crisp on both sides, then with your hand pull
them open, and they will be like a honeycomb;
lay in as much butter as you intend to use,
then clap them together again, and set it by
the fire. When you think the butter is melted
turn them, that both sides may be buttered
alike, but don't touch them with the knife,
either to spread or cut them open, if you do
they will be as heavy as lead, only when they
are quite buttered and done, you may cut them
cross with a knife.[65]

When they were to be served at tea, muffins and crumpets

might be made from a softer dough, as directed by Mrs.

Raffald:

To make TEA CRUMPETS.

    Beat two eggs very well, put to them a
quart of warm milk and water, and a large spoonful of barm; beat in as much fine flour as will
make them rather thicker than a common batter
pudding, then make your bake-stone very hot,
and rub it with a little butter wrapped in a
clean linen cloth, then pour a large spoonful
of batter upon your stone, and let it run to
the size of a tea saucer; turn it, and when
you want to use them toast them very crisp and
butter them.[66]

At the end of the century these British muffins and

---

65. Glasse, Art of Cookery, pp. 298-299.

66. Raffald, English House-keeper, pp. 279-280.

crumpets were still being made in Virginia,[67] along with

a local version:

APOQUINIMINC CAKES.

Put a little salt, one egg beaten, and
four ounces of butter in a quart of flour--
make it into a paste with new milk, beat it
for half an hour with a pestle, roll the paste
thin, and cut it into round cakes; bake them
on a gridiron, and be careful not to burn them.[68]

There was also a colonial adaptation of the baking-

stone--the weeding hoe (the common or broad hoe of inven-

tories) used for the hoecake often described by visitors.

When the tutor Philip Fithian ate it for supper at Nomini

Hall, he enjoyed it and noted that it was "so called be-

cause baked on a Hoe before the fire."[69] The Englishman

J. F. D. Smyth, on the other hand, found it "extremely

harsh and unpleasant" and explained that it was made of

"Indian corn, ground into meal, kneaded into dough, and

baked on a hot, broad, iron hoe."[70] Thomas Anburey

---

67. Randolph, Virginia Housewife, p. 139.

68. Ibid., pp. 139-140. St. George Tucker described
a breakfast party in 1795 where these cakes were featured.
Tucker to William Nelson, July 9, 1795, Tucker-Coleman Papers, College of William and Mary. CW M-1021-9. Cf. a
recipe from Tucker's daughter's collection in Helen Bullock,
The Williamsburg Art of Cookery (Williamsburg, 1939), p. 88.

69. Hunter D. Farish, ed., Journal & Letters of
Philip Vickers Fithian, 1773-1774: A Plantation Tutor of
the Old Dominion (Williamsburg, 1943), p. 74.

70. J. F. D. Smyth, A Tour in the United States of
America... (2 vols., London, 1784), I, 48.

thought that only slaves ate it.[71] It is true that no

contemporary recipe for the Southern version is known.

Amelia Simmons thought it identical with the New England

Johnny cake, which contained flour, milk and molasses,[72]

but contemporary comment and nineteenth-century tradition

place it closer to corn pone, corn dodgers, and ashcake.

All these varieties in Southern cuisine are unsweetened

and unleavened; they are made of corn meal, salt and

shortening, mixed with water and shaped with the hands to

resemble buns. Whether baked before the fire on a hoe,

or a stone, or a board, or a griddle, or in an oven, or

directly in hot ashes, the product is hard, dry and crusty

and it is eaten buttered like Mrs. Glasse's muffins.

---

71. Thomas Anburey, _Travels through the Interior Parts of America_...(2 vols., London, 1789), II, 194, 335.

72. Mary T. Watson, ed., _American Cookery, by Amelia Simmons_ (facs. of 1796 edn., New York, 1958), p. 34.

VI. SAUCES, GARNISHES AND MADE DISHES

The highly stylized repertoire of sauces which dis-
tinguishes la grande cuisine was not established as a convention even in France until the beginning of the nineteenth
century; yet eighteenth-century sauces already had national
characteristics which reflected national tastes.[1] Moreover,
epicures everywhere judged the artistry of individual cooks
by the suitability of their sauces, and a talented housewife might earn a reputation as a discriminating hostess
through the exercise of personal ingenuity in the range and
color of the sauces and garnishes that decorated her dishes.

Sauces were important because scarcely a main dish
was served without them, either poured over the viand or
sent to the table in a separate sauce boat. As Mrs. Bradley
phrased the axiom: "It is to little Purpose that a Servant
knows how to roast and boil if she cannot make the common

---

1. Antonin Carême (1784-1833), the founder of clas-
sic French cookery, was especially interested in sauces,
and the modern French repertoire of 200 great sauces is
largely made up of his inventions and adaptations of old
French, English, Dutch, Italian, Spanish, Portuguese, German, Polish and Russian national sauces. Many of his recipes may be found in Prosper Montagné, Larousse Gastronomique:
The Encyclopedia of Food, Wine & Cookery, ed. by Charlotte
Turgeon and Nina Froud (New York, 1961).

Sauce that is to be sent up with her Meat or Fowls."[2]

The common or conventional sauces in English cookery were gravy, butter, bread, egg, celery, onion, mushroom, and white sauces. The basic ingredient in nearly all of them was gravy--the liquid from a boiled viand or the drippings from a roast. Most housewives kept on hand a supplementary stock of gravy similar to modern consommé, which was prepared by stewing chopped meat with root vegetables, herbs and spices, then straining out the solid ingredients.[3] "Nice" cooks also skimmed off the fat, though they might add butter later. The most useful stock "essence" was made from veal or ham, but bits of other meats, fowls and fish were regularly placed in a stock pot as they became available. Fish stock was usually prepared separately and was not generally used in dressings for meat or fowl; a fish sauce, however, was often reinforced with a strong meat essence.

A simple gravy sauce could be prepared quickly by adding liquid to the drippings or broth--stock gravy, perhaps, or wine--and a thickening agent--bread crumbs, egg

---

2. Martha Bradley, The British Housewife... (London, [c. 1770]), p. 45.

3. Ibid., pp. 47, 238; Mary Randolph, The Virginia Housewife... (Philadelphia, 1855), pp. 90-91; [Hannah Glasse], The Art of Cookery... (7th edn., London, 1760), pp. ii-iii, 18, 19; Sarah Harrison, The House-keeper's

yolks, or pieces of butter rolled in flour. (French cooks were making roux, in the accepted modern manner, but the English preferred to roll bits of butter in flour and drop them into the hot liquid.) Additional seasonings popular for general use included salt and pepper, other spices, horseradish, mustard, walnut or mushroom catsup, parsley and other herbs. If the viand was a fowl, its liver might be brayed and added to the gravy for both thickening and flavor. For wild game, either vinegar, verjuice, or lemon might be substituted for white wine. For fish and seafood, the stock might be augmented with oysters in their juice, or chopped anchovies, minced shrimp or lobster, and seasoned with pickled capers, catsup or lemon.

Butter sauce was still popular, though it tended to smother the flavor of the viand it embellished and contributed more than its share to the "greasy" reputation of English sauces. "There is more Nicety in melting Butter well, than is commonly imagined," warned Mrs. Bradley, "and nothing is more vexatious than to have it ill done."[4] Mrs. Randolph agreed:

TO MELT BUTTER.
Nothing is more simple than this process, and nothing so generally done badly. Keep a

---

Pocket-book... (6th edn., London, 1755), pp. 126-128.

4. Bradley, British Housewife, p. 47.

quart tin sauce-pan, with a cover to it, exclusively for this purpose; weigh one quarter of
a pound of good butter; rub into it two tea-
spoonsful of flour; when well mixed, put it in
the sauce-pan with one table-spoonful of water,
and a little salt; cover it, and set the sauce-
pan in a larger one of boiling water; shake it
constantly till completely melted, and beginning
to boil. If the pan containing the butter be
set on coals, it will oil the butter and spoil it.
This quantity is sufficient for one sauce-boat.[5]

The popularity of this sauce stemmed from its versa-
tility:

A great variety of delicious sauces can
be made, by adding different herbs to melted
butter, all of which are excellent to eat with
fish, poultry, or boiled butchers' meat. To
begin with parsley--wash a large bunch very
clean, pick the leaves from the stems carefully, boil them ten minutes in salt and water,
drain them perfectly dry, mince them exceedingly fine, and stir them in the butter when
it begins to melt. When herbs are added to
butter, you must put two spoonsful of water
instead of one. Chervil, young fennel, burnet,
tarragon, and cress, or pepper-grass, may all
be used, and must be prepared in the same
manner as parsley.[6]

Bread sauce, equally English in character,[7] was used

in Virginia as Mrs. Randolph directed:

Cut the crumb of a loaf of bread in thin
slices, and put it in cold water with a few
pepper corns, a little salt and onion--then

---

5. Randolph, Virginia Housewife, pp. 93-94.

6. Ibid., p. 94; cf. Elizabeth Raffald, The Experienced English House-keeper... (4th edn., London, 1775), p. 24.

7. It is still so labeled in Larousse Gastronomique,
p. 852.

boil it till the bread is quite soft, beat it
well, put in a quarter of a pound of butter,
two spoonsful of thick cream, and put it in
the dish with the [roast] turkey.[8]

It was suitable also for other poultry and for small game

birds.[9] Mrs. Bradley and Mrs. Glasse recommended it for

larks,[10] and Mrs. Raffald used it to accompany a roast pig.[11]

Egg sauce, usually served with a large fowl but in

a separate sauce dish, was prepared from hard-boiled eggs,

chopped and added to melted butter. The proportions could

vary, but the mixture had to be "thick and fine"; about

four eggs to a quarter of a pound of butter would produce

the desired consistency.[12] Mrs. Raffald suggested also

that it be served very hot, poured over a salt codfish.

Celery sauce was usually poured over the viand--

either boiled or roast fowl, game birds, veal or mutton.

It was prepared by stewing chopped celery gently until it

---

8. Randolph, Virginia Housewife, pp. 72-73; Raffald,
English House-keeper, pp. 62-63.

9. Larousse Gastronomique, p. 852. The French prepared it in heated milk instead of water and used only two
tablespoons of butter and half a cup of cream, making it
smoother and lighter.

10. Bradley, British Housewife, p. 235; Glasse, Art
of Cookery, pp. 5-6.

11. Raffald, English House-keeper, p. 56.

12. Glasse, Art of Cookery, pp. 67, 68; Bradley,
British Housewife, p. 46; Raffald, English House-keeper,
pp. 23, 64; Randolph, Virginia Housewife, p. 74.

was tender, then adding cream, thickening with butter rolled
in flour, and seasoning it with salt and pepper, mace and
nutmeg. There were several popular substitutes for the
cream: the water in which the celery was stewed, or white
wine, or stock gravy. Mrs. Glasse and Mrs. Bradley suggested the use of catsup for additional flavor.[13]

While onions were generously used in many gravy
sauces, there was a special onion sauce to go with boiled
goose or duck, roasted rabbit or mutton. Whole onions were
boiled until tender, then strained and chopped, returned to
the saucepan and reheated with enough cream and butter to
give the sauce a thick, smooth texture.[14] If shallots were
used instead of onions, it was necessary only to mince them
and simmer them briefly in a thin gravy or in a mixture of
equal parts of white wine, water and vinegar.[15]

Mushrooms, like onions, were often added to gravy
sauces, and in the conventional English repertoire there
was a special mushroom sauce for fowls. Whole fresh mushrooms were carefully washed and heated in a saucepan with

---

13. Glasse, Art of Cookery, pp. 67, 68; Bradley,
British Housewife, pp. 46, 165-166; Raffald, English House-
keeper, p. 105; Randolph, Virginia Housewife, pp. 92-93.

14. Glasse, Art of Cookery, p. 9; Raffald, English
House-keeper, p. 59; Randolph, Virginia Housewife, pp. 91-92.

15. Glasse, Art of Cookery, p. 68; Bradley, British
Housewife, p. 329.

cream, thickened with butter rolled in flour, and seasoned
with salt, nutmeg and mace.[16] Mrs. Randolph prepared a
similar sauce but sliced the mushrooms and sautéed them
in butter before adding the cream; and she used egg yolks
instead of floured butter for thickening.[17]

The English white sauce, "rich and thick," was served
on fowl or roasted hare. Mrs. Glasse and Mrs. Bradley
made it by heating together a pint of cream and half a
pound of butter, stirring it steadily until it reached
a heavy, smooth consistency.[18] Mrs. Raffald and Mrs.
Randolph prepared it from a stock gravy base:

TO MAKE WHITE SAUCE FOR FOWLS.

Take a scrag of veal, the necks of fowls,
or any bits of mutton or veal you have; put
them in a sauce pan with a blade or two of
mace, a few black pepper corns, one anchovy,
a head of celery, a bunch of sweet herbs, a
slice of the end of a lemon; put in a quart
of water, cover it close, let it boil till
it is reduced to half a pint, strain it, and
thicken it with a quarter of a pound of butter
mixed with flour, boil it five or six minutes,
put in two spoonsful of pickled mushrooms, mix
the yelks of two eggs with a tea cup full of
good cream and a little nutmeg--put it in the
sauce, keep shaking it over the fire, but
don't let it boil.[19]

---

16. Glasse, _Art of Cookery_, p. 67; Bradley, _British Housewife_, pp. 46, 420.

17. Randolph, _Virginia Housewife_, p. 93.

18. Glasse, _Art of Cookery_, p. 7; Bradley, _British Housewife_, p. 235.

19. Randolph, _Virginia Housewife_, p. 73; Raffald,

But Mrs. Randolph also prepared a white sauce from a roux

(suitably labeled SAUCE A-LA-CREME) and served it in an

egg dish:

> Put a quarter of a pound of butter, with
> a large tablespoonful of flour rubbed well into
> it in a sauce pan; add some chopped parsley, a
> little onion, salt, pepper, nutmeg, and a gill
> of cream; stir it over the fire until it be-
> gins to boil, then pour it over the eggs....[20]

These eight common sauces belonged to "the Rudiments

of Cookery." For "the Practice of the Art in its full

Perfection" a more extensive repertoire of equally Brit-

ish sauces was required "to answer the Demand of the most

elegant Tables."[21]

There was apple sauce for goose, prepared as we make

it today and served in a separate china bowl.[22] Orange

sauce, made by adding orange juice to a gravy, was poured

over ducks and wild fowl.[23] A green sauce was used with

lamb, but it was not the modern mint jelly; Mrs. Harrison

and Mrs. Randolph prepared it with fresh mint chopped fine,

mixed with enough vinegar to make it liquid and sweetened

English House-keeper, p. 63.

20. Randolph, Virginia Housewife, p. 87.

21. Bradley, British Housewife, p. 327.

22. Raffald, English House-keeper, p. 59; Randolph, Virginia Housewife, p. 70.

23. Bradley, British Housewife, p. 328; Randolph, Virginia Housewife, p. 79.

with sugar.[24] Mrs. Bradley's green sauce got its color

from young green wheat crushed in a mortar, and Mrs. Har-

rison also used chopped spinach and parsley.[25] Venison,

like wild fowl, was traditionally accompanied by a sweet-

sour sauce preferably red in color.[26]

For different kinds of fish and seafood there was

less specialization in the accompanying sauces. Mrs. Ran-

dolph's "FISH SAUCE, TO KEEP A YEAR" described their gen-

eral character:

> Chop twenty-four anchovies, bones and all,
> ten shallots, a handful of scraped horse rad-
> ish, four blades of mace, one quart of white
> wine, one pint of anchovy liquor, one pint of
> claret, twelve cloves, and twelve pepper corns;
> boil them together till reduced to a quart,
> then strain it off into a bottle for use. Two
> spoonsful will be sufficient for a pound of
> butter.[27]

When shellfish was available, it was freely used in

fish sauce; oysters, shrimp and lobster were especially

valued for this purpose. In Virginia the tidewater rivers

---

24. Harrison, Pocket-book, p. 107; Randolph, Virginia Housewife, p. 44.

25. Bradley, British Housewife, pp. 328-329; Harrison, Pocket-book, p. 132. For another traditional green sauce, made of gooseberries and served with green goose, see above p. 81 and Raffald, English House-keeper, p. 58.

26. For recommended ingredients see above p. 81.

27. Randolph, Virginia Housewife, p. 90; cf. Sturgeon, pp. 68-69.

yielded oysters the year round, and they were large, suc-

culent and plentiful. Landon Carter of Sabine Hall often

had them harvested twenty bushels at a time, serving part

of them immediately--either raw, stewed, in fritters or

"for Sauces of all kinds"--and pickling a few bushels for

later use.[28] To prepare the sauce for fish Mrs. Randolph

directed:

> Scald a pint of oysters, and strain them
> through a sieve; then wash some more in cold
> water, and take off their beards; put them in
> a stew-pan, and pour the liquor over them;
> then add a large spoonful of anchovy liquor,
> half a lemon, two blades of mace, and thicken
> it with butter rolled in flour. Put in half
> a pound of butter, and boil it till it is
> melted--take out the mace and lemon, and
> squeeze the lemon juice into the sauce; boil
> it, and stir it all the time, and put it in
> a boat.[29]

In England and in Virginia a similar oyster sauce

was served with boiled turkey:

> As you open the oysters, put a pint
> into a bowl, wash them out of their own
> liquor, and put them in another bowl; when
> the liquor has settled, pour it off into a

---

28. Jack P. Greene, ed., The Diary of Colonel Landon
Carter of Sabine Hall, 1752-1778 (2 vols., Charlottesville,
1965), II, 861, 1062. The numerous additional references
to oysters show that Carter harvested them in January, February, March, April, May July, September, October and December, and he tells us that he ate them in July without
ill effects though his neighbors usually observed the
traditional summer proscription.

29. Randolph, Virginia Housewife, p. 92. Glasse,
Art of Cookery, p. 119, is similar but she uses gravy too.

sauce pan with a little white gravy, and a
teaspoonful of lemon pickle--thicken it with
flour and a good lump of butter; boil it three
or four minutes, put in a spoonful of good
cream, add the oysters, keep shaking them over
the fire till they are quite hot, but don't
let them boil, for it will make them hard and
appear small.[30]

Lobster, shrimp and cockle sauces were usually made

by adding cooked pieces of the shellfish to a basic butter

sauce:

Take a lobster, if it be alive, stick a
skewer in the rent of the tail, (to keep the
water out,) throw a handful of salt in the
water; when it boils, put in the lobster, and
boil it half an hour; if it has spawn on it,
pick them off, and pound them exceedingly fine
in a marble mortar, and put them into half a
pound of good melted butter, then take the
meat out of the lobster, pull it in bits, and
put it in your butter, with a meat spoonful of
lemon pickle, and the same of walnut catsup,
a slice of lemon, one or two slices of horse-
radish, a little beaten mace, salt and cayenne
to your taste; boil them one minute, then take
out the horse-radish and lemon, and serve it up
in your sauce boat.

N. B. If you cannot get lobsters, you may
make shrimp, cockle, or muscle sauce, the same
way; if there can be no shell fish got, you
then may add two anchovies cut small, a spoonful of walnut liquor, a large onion stuck with
cloves--strain and put it in the sauce boat.[31]

Mrs. Glasse permitted the use of beef gravy but did not

recommend it:

---

30. Ibid., p. 72. Raffald, English House-keeper,
p. 61, is identical.

31. Randolph, Virginia Housewife, pp. 61-62; Raffald, English House-keeper, p. 21.

If you would have your sauce very rich,
let one half be rich beef gravy, and the other
half melted butter with the lobster; but the
gravy, I think, takes away the sweetness of
the butter and lobster, and the fine flavour
of the fish.[32]

To add variety to her meat dishes the housewife was
advised to serve different sauces from day to day and to
offer more than one with each viand. Yet the cookbooks
suggested few specific variations: with roast goose,
gravy sauce in one basin and applesauce in another; with
the gravy sauce poured over fowls, turkeys, ducks, pheasants, partridges or larks, separate basins of bread sauce,
egg sauce or onion sauce.[33] She was apparently expected
to achieve her own variety with ingenious or original seasonings in the gravy.

While everyone recognized the superior quality and
range of French sauces, they were considered too extravagantly expensive for ordinary families. Their chief virtue,
according to Mrs. Bradley, was "that they do not spoil the
Taste of the Meat, which we drown and overwhelm with our
several thick Sauces with Butter."[34] Since her readers
were expected to share her distrust of French chefs, who
"beggared" the great families they served, she proposed to

---

32. Glasse, Art of Cookery, p. 119.

33. Ibid., p. 5; Harrison, Pocket-book, pp. 85-107.

34. Bradley, British Housewife, p. 421.

duplicate their elegance "at a moderate Price,"[35] for example, with "Poverade":

> Put into a Saucepan half a Pint of Vinegar, and four Table Spoonfuls of Veal Gravy, add to this three good Slices of Lemon, an Onion cut to Pieces, and a whole Leek; season it with Salt, and add a good deal of whole Pepper.
> Set this on the Fire to boil gently for some Time, and when it is enough strain it through a Sieve into a Sauce Boat, and send it up hot.[36]

Mrs. Bradley claimed too much, for no Frenchman would have recognized her barbarism. A French chef made Poivrade this way: First he simmered over very low heat a good consommé seasoned with lean ham, carrot, onion, a pinch of several spices and two tablespoons of vinegar. Next he added fresh consommé and half a cup of Espagnole (a finished basic sauce of meat stock, white wine, and tomato juice thickened with a seasoned roux or mirepoix) and simmered this mixture a few minutes. Then he strained the sauce and reduced it to the desired consistency instead of thickening it, and added a little butter just before serving it.[37] The French secret was not so much

---

35. Ibid., p. 327.

36. Ibid., p. 421. For similar sauces see Glasse, Art of Cookery, Chapter III, "Read this Chapter, and you will find how expensive a French cook's sauce is," pp. 103-106. Her contempt for French sauces is even greater: "This dish I do not recommend; for I think it an odd jumble of trash.... I think here is enough to shew the folly of these fine French cooks."

37. Carême's recipe as translated in Larousse

extravagance as care and imagination.

From limited evidence it may be concluded that Virginia tastes in sauces were very British. In Mrs. Custis's book of cookery only three recipes for sauces are given separately. For a capon she recommended mixing oysters in their liquor with ale and claret, adding bread crumbs, onion, lemon peel, salt and the inevitable piece of butter.[38] Her hen sauce was made of mutton gravy, minced hard-cooked eggs, mustard, and lemon juice or vinegar, all heated together.[39] Another sauce for use with any fowl, wild or domestic, was prepared from strong broth and claret, grated bread crumbs, minced lemon and anchovy.[40] Like Mrs. Randolph's, her sauces are very close to those of Mrs. Smith and Mrs. Glasse, without any of the French influence admired by Mrs. Bradley.

Thomas Jefferson, accustomed to this English lack of subtlety in Virginia, was especially delighted with French sauces when he first came to know them in Paris. Back home at Monticello, in Philadelphia and in Washington he used hachée, tournée, piquante, and Robert among others.[41]

Gastronomique, p. 828.

38. Frances Parke Custis, A Booke of Cookery, No. 22.

39. Ibid., No. 23.

40. Ibid., No. 24.

41. Marie Kimball, Thomas Jefferson's Cook Book (Richmond, 1949), pp. 30-33.

These "foreign" sauces, like his wine cellar, contributed

to his reputation as a gourmet and earned Patrick Henry's

famous dictum, that he had "abjured his native vittles."

For the proper dressing of main dishes, garnishes

were almost as important as sauces.[42] Sliced lemon could

be used with anything and was especially suitable for fish.

Sippets were popular decorations for dishes with sauce

poured over the viand. To make pretty sippets, thin slices

of bread were cut into strips, triangles or circles and

either toasted or fried in butter.[43] Hard-cooked eggs,

minced, became part of the sauce when the dish was served;

sliced or halved, they kept their separate identity.[44]

Sliced bacon, fried into crisp curls, was equally versa-

tile for decoration and had the additional virtue of a

contrasting flavor. Fresh parsley and other herbs from

---

42. The cookbooks usually suggest suitable garnishes
as part of the recipe. For conventional garnishes see Harrison, Pocket-book, pp. 85-107; Glasse, Art of Cookery,
pp. 21-62; E. Smith, The Compleat Housewife... (Williamsburg, 1742), pp. 10-30; Raffald, English House-keeper, pp.
21-65, 79-143; Bradley, British Housewife, separate chapter on Made Dishes for each month; Randolph, Virginia
Housewife, pp. 29-69; Custis, Booke of Cookery, No. 1-7,
13-18, 29, 37, 45, 182-200.

43. "Fried toasts" might be a dessert dish, made
of bread soaked in a sweet custard mixture, spiced, then
fried and served in a wine sauce. Raffald, English House-
keeper, p. 263.

44. Mrs. Custis in recipe No. 200 used only the
yolks, carefully halved.

the kitchen garden added color to the dish, whether served
in crisp sprigs or chopped or wilted or fried.[45] Scraped
horseradish was popular for roasts of all kinds and for
fish. For winter use, when other garnishes might be un-
available, pickled capers, barberries, walnuts, or vegetables and fruits of various kinds were recommended.[46]

For greater elegance there were favorite combinations
of separately prepared foods that could be served together
in one dish. A small roast, either flesh or fowl, might
be sent to the table surrounded by small fried sausages or
forcemeat balls. A large fish, boiled with care to preserve its shape, might be placed in the center of a large
platter and the edges covered with roe (fried or boiled),
or lumps of lobster meat, fried oysters, small fried fish
(about the size of smelts), or patties like these suggested
by Mrs. Raffald:

To make LOBSTER PATTIES to garnish FISH.
Take all the red seeds and meat of a lobster, with a little pepper, salt, and crumbs
of bread, mix them well with a little butter,
make them up in small patties, and put them in
either rich batter or thin paste, fry or bake
them, and garnish your fish with them.[47]

---

45. The French still use fried parsley as a garnish for fried dishes. Sprigs or single leaves are washed
and dried, then fried quickly in butter or in sizzling
deep fat; for a recipe see Larousse Gastronomique, p. 700.

46. See Chapter VII.

47. Raffald, English House-keeper, p. 41; cf.

In Virginia, oysters were fried without batter and served with things other than fish:

TO FRY OYSTERS.

Take a quarter of a hundred of large oysters, wash them and roll them in grated bread,
with pepper and salt, and fry them a light
brown; if you choose, you may add a little parsley, shred fine. They are a proper garnish
for calves' head, or most made dishes.[48]

Many of the more elaborate garnishes, prepared in

larger size or quantity, could be used as side dishes;

for example, oyster loaves:

Take little round loaves, cut off the
tops, scrape out all the crumbs, then put the
oysters into a stew pan with the crumbs that
came out of the loaves, a little water, and a
good lump of butter; stew them together ten
or fifteen minutes, then put in a spoonful of
good cream, fill your loaves, lay the bit of
crust carefully on again, set them in the oven
to crisp. Three are enough for a side dish.[49]

When a main dish was composed of several basic ingre-

dients and when its accompanying sauces and garnishes were

elaborate, it was called a made dish and considered suit-

able for the most formal occasion. The cohesive agent in

most dishes was either English white sauce or a brown gravy

Bradley, British Housewife, pp. 357-358.

48. Randolph, Virginia Housewife, p. 69; cf. Raffald, English House-keeper, p. 39, where a spiced batter
is used.

49. Ibid. Cf. Smith, Compleat Housewife, p.8; Harrison, Pocket-book, p. 61; Raffald, English House-keeper,
p. 40; Bradley, British Housewife, p. 172.

sauce, thick and highly seasoned. Cookbooks emphasized the importance of a sauce that was smooth and clear. For white sauce Mrs. Raffald directed:

> Be careful the tossing pan is well tinned,
> quite clean, and not gritty, and put every in-
> gredient into your white sauce, and have it of
> a proper thickness, and well boiled, before
> you put in eggs and cream, for they will not
> add much to the thickness, nor stir them with
> a spoon after they are in, nor set your pan on
> the fire, for it will gather at the bottom and
> be in lumps, but hold your pan a good height
> from the fire, and keep shaking the pan round
> one way, it will keep the sauce from curdling,
> and be sure you don't let it boil; it is the
> best way to take up your meat, collops, or
> hash, or any other kind of dish you are making
> with a fish slice, and strain your sauce upon
> it, for it is almost impossible to prevent
> little bits of meat from mixing with the sauce,
> and by this method the sauce will look clear.[50]

"And as to brown sauce," wrote Mrs. Glasse, "take great care no fat swims at the top, but that it be all smooth alike, and about as thick as good cream, and not to taste of one thing more than another."[51] Mrs. Raffald urged special care with wine and fresh anchovy, that each of these troublesome ingredients be "put in some time before your dish is ready, to take off the rawness."[52]

---

50. Raffald, English House-keeper, pp. 79-80.

51. Glasse, Art of Cookery, p. 103.

52. Raffald, English House-keeper, p. 80; cf. Martha (Jefferson) Randolph's rules in Kimball, Jefferson's Cook Book, p. 52.

A general rule for adding solids to the sauce was

stated by Mrs. Glasse:

> As to most made-dishes, you may put in
> what you think proper to enlarge it, or make
> it good; as mushrooms pickled, dried, fresh,
> or powdered; truffles, morels, cocks combs
> stewed, ox palates cut in little bits, arti-
> choke-bottoms, either pickled, fresh boiled,
> or dried ones softened in warm water, each cut
> in four pieces, asparagus-tops, the yolks of
> hard eggs, force-meat-balls, &c. The best
> things to give a sauce a tartness, are mush-
> room-pickle, white walnut-pickle, elder vine-
> gar, or lemon-juice.[53]

For the forcemeat balls so often used as a garnish,

she offered an all-purpose recipe:

> Now you are to observe, that force-meat
> balls are a great addition to all made-dishes;
> made thus: take half a pound of veal, and
> half a pound of sewet, cut fine, and beat in
> a marble mortar or wooden bowl; have a few
> sweet herbs shred fine, a little mace dried
> and beat fine, a small nutmeg grated, or half
> a large one, a little lemon-peel cut very fine,
> a little pepper and salt, and the yolks of two
> eggs; mix all these well together, then roll
> them in little round balls, and some in little
> long balls; roll them in flour, and fry them
> brown. If they are for any thing of white
> sauce, put a little water on in a sauce-pan,
> and when the water boils put them in, and let
> them boil for a few minutes, but never fry
> them for white sauce.[54]

When the balls were added to the sauce, as Mrs. Raffald

directed, they were first fried, then placed in a sieve

---

53. Glasse, Art of Cookery, p. 103; Mrs. Raffald
has a similar list, p. 80.

54. Glasse, Art of Cookery, pp. 21-22; Mrs. Randolph's recipe, p. 91, is almost identical.

"to drain the fat from them"; they should never be allowed to "boil in your sauce" because "it will give them a greasy look, and soften the balls." Indeed, "the best way is to put them in after your meat is dished up."[55]

Since made dishes connoted elegance, the authors of cookbooks took pains to offer their readers a number of variations on current innovations in the British repertoire. French names carried special appeal--ragouts, fricassees, dishes à la mode, à la daube, à la braise, for example. In all these, large cuts of meat were either boned, sliced or coarsely chopped and fowls were jointed before being stewed or browned; then the pieces were reheated in the sauce, which contained mushrooms and other vegetable ingredients as well as a variety of flavoring agents.

The meats for a ragout were usually browned, either by roasting or frying, and served in a thick brown gravy sauce. These are typical recipes:

To ragoo a Breast of Veal.

Half roast a breast of veal, then bone it and put it in a tossing pan, with a quart of veal gravy, one ounce of morels, the same of truffles, stew it till tender, and just before you thicken the gravy, put in a few oysters, pickled mushrooms, and pickled cucumbers, cut in small square pieces, the yolks of four eggs boiled hard, cut your sweetbread in slices, and fry it a light brown, dish up your meal, and pour the gravy hot over it, lay your sweet-

---

55. Raffald, English House-keeper, p. 80.

bread round, morels, truffles, and eggs upon
it: garnish with pickled barberries; this is
proper for either top or side for dinner, or
bottom for supper [56]

To ragoo a piece of beef.

Take a large piece of the flank, which has
fat at the top cut square, or any piece that
is all meat, and has fat at the top, but no
bones. The rump does well. Cut all nicely
off the bone (which makes fine soup) then take
a large stew-pan, and with a good piece of
butter fry it a little brown all over, flour-
ing your meat well before you put it into the
pan, then pour in as much gravy as will cover
it, made thus: take about a pound of coarse
beef, a little piece of veal cut small, a bundle of sweet herbs, an onion, some whole black
pepper and white pepper, two or three large
blades of mace, four or five cloves, a piece
of carrot, a little piece of bacon steeped in
vinegar a little while, a crust of bread
toasted brown; put to this a quart of water,
and let it boil till half wasted. While this
is making, pour a quart of boiling water into
the stew-pan, cover it close, and let it be
stewing softly; when the gravy is done strain
it, pour it into the pan where the beef is,
take an ounce of truffles and morels cut small,
some fresh or dried mushrooms cut small, two
spoonfuls of catchup, and cover it close. Let
all this stew till the sauce is rich and thick:
then have ready some artichoke bottoms cut into
four, and a few pickled mushrooms, give them a
boil or two, and when your meat is tender and
your sauce quite rich, lay the meat into a dish
and pour the sauce over it. You may add a
sweetbread cut in six pieces, a palate stewed
tender cut into little pieces, some cocks-combs,
and a few force-meat balls. These are a great
addition, but it will be good without.

Note, for variety, when the beef is ready
and the gravy put to it, add a large bunch of

---

56. _Ibid._, p. 90; Mrs. Randolph's recipe, p. 37,
is similar but she uses red wine and curry powder as
additional seasonings.

sellery cut small and washed clean, two spoonfuls of catchup, and a glass of red wine. Omit
all the other ingredients. When the meat and
sellery are tender, and the sauce rich and good,
serve it up. It is also very good this way:
take six large cucumbers, scoop out the seeds,
pare them, cut them into slices, and do them
just as you do the sellery.[57]

A brown fricassee was usually prepared like a ragout;
in fact, the two terms were often used interchangeably. A
white fricassee--especially suitable for small fowls, rabbits, lamb, veal and other white meats--was made with a
white sauce. When the meat was pre-cooked, it was generally
stewed with herbs and other seasonings; the broth was then
strained and used in the sauce. One of Mrs. Glasse's basic
recipes suggested the following proportions: to a cup of
broth, a cup of cream, the yolks of two eggs, half a nutmeg
grated, a glass of white wine, a gill of mushrooms, a little
piece of butter rolled in flour. When the sauce was "smooth
and of a fine thickness," you might "add what you please."[58]

In Virginia the sauces for ragouts and fricassees
were simpler but as widely used. Mrs. Randolph fricasseed
chickens, calves' feet, or cod sounds in a smooth, clear
sauce without mushrooms or other vegetables; forcemeat

---

57. Glasse, Art of Cookery, pp. 33-34; cf. Bradley,
British Housewife, pp. 53-55; Harrison, Pocket-book, pp.
36-38.

58. Ibid., p. 23.

balls and other solids were added as garnishes.[59] She
ragouted traditional cuts of veal, mutton, and pigs'
feet.[60] Though she did not use the term "made dish" several of her recipes fill the conventional requirements.
For example:

TO HARRICO MUTTON.

Take the nicest part of the rack, divide
it into chops, with one bone in each, beat them
flat, sprinkle salt and pepper on them, and
broil them nicely; make a rich gravy out of the
inferior parts, season it well with pepper, a
little spice, and any kind of catsup you choose;
when sufficiently done, strain it, and thicken
it with butter and brown flour, have some carrots and turnips cut into small dice and boiled
till tender, put them in the gravy, lay the
chops in and stew them fifteen minutes; serve
them up garnished with green pickle.[61]

CHICKEN PUDDING, A FAVOURITE VIRGINIA DISH.

Beat ten eggs very light, add to them a
quart of rich milk, with a quarter of a pound
of butter melted, and some pepper and salt;
stir in as much flour as will make a thin good
batter; take four young chickens, and after
cleaning them nicely, cut off the legs, wings,
&c. put them all in a sauce pan, with some
salt and water, and a bundle of thyme and parsley, boil them till nearly done, then take the
chicken from the water and put it in the batter pour it in a deep dish, and bake it; send
nice white gravy in a boat.[62]

---

59. Randolph, _Virginia Housewife_, pp. 41, 65, 74.

60. _Ibid._, pp. 37, 47, 54.

61. _Ibid._, pp. 46-47.

62. _Ibid._, pp. 83-84.

Domestic fowls, ducks, partridges and pheasants could be cooked whole à la braise. The fowl was trussed as for boiling (wild fowl were also larded), then placed in a large saucepan on top of thin layers of sliced veal, beef and bacon, then covered with similar layers. Other seasonings were added--carrot, an onion stuck with cloves, mace, pepper, salt, sweet herbs--and the whole was stewed gently for an hour or so, tightly covered, with enough liquid to fill the pan. When the fowl was tender, it was removed from the broth, which was then strained, thickened, and augmented with wine or cream and a selection of the traditional ingredients of made dishes: mushrooms, livers, sweetbreads, ox palates, cocks' combs, oysters, anchovies, artichokes, celery. Favorite garnishes were forcemeat balls, barberries and lemon.[63]

A rump of beef dressed à la mode was first boned, then larded or stuffed with forcemeat, stewed gently with conventional seasonings, and served with brown gravy similar to a ragout.[64]

When cuts of meat or fowls cooked à la daube were to be served hot, the recipe was only a slight variation

---

63. Glasse, Art of Cookery, pp. 71, 80, 92, 94; Raffald, English House-keeper, pp. 123, 128.

64. Glasse, Art of Cookery, pp. 36-37; Harrison, Pocket-book, p. 38; Raffald, English House-keeper, p. 116;

on à la mode or à la braise; sometimes layers of other

meats were included, and occasionally the meat was browned

before the liquid was added. Served cold, the dish had

real distinction--the accompanying sauce was jelled.[65]

Mrs. Randolph's directions included a separate recipe for

the jelled sauce, which was especially attractive because

it was clear and firm:

TO MAKE SAVOURY JELLY.

Put eight or ten pounds of coarse lean
beef, or the same quantity of the inferior
parts of the fore quarter of veal, into a pot
with two gallons of water, a pound of lean
salt pork, three large onions chopped, three
carrots, a large handful of parsley, and any
sweet herb that you choose, with pepper and
salt; boil it very gently till reduced to two
quarts; strain it through a sieve--next day,
take off the fat, turn out the jelly, and
separate it from the dregs at the bottom; put
it on the fire with half a pint of white wine,
a large spoonful of lemon pickle, and the
whites and shells of four eggs beaten: when it
boils clear on one side, run it through the
jelly bag.[66]

She recommended its use with small birds, roasted whole,

or with roast chicken, quartered, or with a small turkey,

boned and stuffed with forcemeat and boiled with sliced

Randolph, Virginia Housewife, p. 29.

65. For a clear distinction see Mrs. Raffald, "A
TURKEY A-LA-DAUB, to be sent up hot," p. 122, and "TURKEY
A-LA-DAUB, to be sent up cold," p. 123.

66. Randolph, Virginia Housewife, pp. 152-153.

ham or tongue.[67] To make the dish as attractive as possible, she suggested that it be molded in a tureen just large enough to accommodate the fowls and that about an inch and a half of jelly be set firmly in the bottom before the cold fowls were laid in, breasts down; then the tureen ought to be filled "with jelly up to their backs" and care taken "that the birds are not displaced." Just before serving, the dish should be unmolded by setting "it a moment in hot water to loosen it"; then "put the dish on the top, and turn it out carefully."[68] Fish, too, could be prepared à la daube:

> Boil as many large white perch as will be
> sufficient for the dish; do not take off their
> heads, and be careful not to break their skins;
> when cold, place them in the dish, and cover
> them with savoury jelly broken. A nice piece
> of rock-fish is excellent done in the same way.[69]

Another French dish, fricandeau, originally made of loin or rump of veal, larded, then braised or roasted,[70] was adapted for a number of English fricandos. Beef and veal were sliced, larded, then roasted or broiled, then stewed in a highly seasoned broth (like collops) and served with general garnishes--lemon, barberries, forcemeat balls,

---

67. Ibid., pp. 151-153.

68. Ibid., p. 152.

69. Ibid., p. 66.

70. Larousse Gastronomique, p. 430.

egg yolks.[71] Pigeons also were prepared in a similar way:

Pigeons in Fricandos.

After having trussed your pigeons with
their legs in their bodies, divide them in two,
and lard them with bacon; then lay them in a
stew-pan with the larded side downwards, and
two whole leeks cut small, two ladlefuls of
mutton broth, or veal gravy; cover them close
over a very slow fire, and when they are enough
make your fire very brisk, to waste away what
liquor remains: when they are of a fine brown
take them up, and pour out all the fat that is
left in the pan; then pour in some veal gravy
to loosen what sticks to the pan, and a little
pepper; stir it about for two or three minutes
and pour it over the pigeons. This is a pretty
little side-dish.[72]

Slices of beef or veal, beaten flat and rolled up
around forcemeat stuffing, then browned, were served with
a gravy or ragout as "olives" like modern "birds." Mrs.
Randolph roasted them and stewed them in the gravy as
follows:

BEEF OLIVES.

Cut slices from a fat rump of beef six
inches long and half an inch thick, beat them
well with a pestle; make a forcemeat of bread
crumbs, fat bacon chopped, parsley, a little
onion, some shred suet, pounded mace, pepper
and salt; mix it up with the yelks of eggs,
and spread a thin layer over each slice of
beef, roll it up tight, and secure the rolls
with skewers, set them before the fire, and
turn them till they are a nice brown; have

---

71. Raffald, English House-keeper, pp. 94, 115;
Randolph, Virginia Housewife, p. 30.

72. Glasse, Art of Cookery, p. 88; cf. Raffald,
English House-keeper, p. 132.

ready a pint of good gravy, thickened with
brown flour and a spoonful of butter, a gill
of red wine, with two spoonsful of mushroom
catsup, lay the rolls in it, and stew them
till tender; garnish with forcemeat balls.[73]

Other recipes recommended frying or baking the rolls and

serving them with mushrooms, sweetbreads, oysters, or

hard-cooked egg yolks in the gravy sauce--a side dish

suitable for the second course.[74]

The name of the French poupeton (a meat roll similar

to olives, usually braised)[75] was borrowed for a dish of

pigeons, called a "Pulpatoon" by Mrs. Smith, a "Pompetone"

by Mrs. Harrison, and by Mrs. Glasse:

A French pupton of pigeons.

Take savoury force-meat rolled out like
paste, put it in a buttered dish, lay a layer
of very thin bacon, squab pigeons, sliced sweetbread, asparagus-tops, mushrooms, cocks combs, a
palate boiled tender and cut into pieces, and the
yolks of hard eggs; make another force-meat and
lay over like a pie, bake it, and when enough
turn it into a dish, and pour gravy round it.[76]

In an effort to suggest original and elegant crea-

tions, each cookbook offered its own special extravaganzas.

---

73. Randolph, Virginia Housewife, pp. 29-30.

74. Glasse, Art of Cookery, pp. 37, 54, 55; Raffald, English House-keeper, pp. 94, 95, 117; Randolph,
Virginia Housewife, p. 37.

75. Larousse Gastronomique, p. 771.

76. Glasse, Art of Cookery, p. 87; cf. Smith, Compleat Housewife, p. 59; Harrison, Pocket-book, p. 195.

Mrs. Glasse's pigeons transmogrified, for example, were
relatively simple: dressed as for roasting, they were
wrapped in enough puff paste to disguise them, then boiled
in a cloth to preserve their shape, and served in a clear
gravy sauce.[77] But Mrs. Raffald's transformation would
indeed astonish the beholder:

> PIGEONS transmogrified.
>
> Pick and clean six small young pigeons,
> but do not cut off their heads, cut off their
> pinions, and boil them ten minutes in water,
> then cut off the ends of six large cucumbers
> and scrape out the seeds, put in your pigeons,
> but let the heads be cut [put?] at the ends of
> the cucumbers, and stick a bunch of barberries
> in their bills, and then put them into a toss-
> ing-pan with a pint of veal gravy, a little an-
> chovy, a glass of red wine, a spoonful of brown-
> ing, a little slice of lemon, Chyan [cayenne]
> and salt to your taste, stew them seven minutes,
> take them out, thicken your gravy with a little
> butter rolled in flour, boil it up and strain
> it over your pigeons, and serve it up.[78]

The fabled showpiece of medieval Christmas dinners--
the boar's head--no longer graced English tables[79] but
calf's head was still a popular "top" dish for any season
of the year. Boned, stuffed with forcemeat, and carefully

---

77. Glasse, Art of Cookery, p. 88.

78. Raffald, English House-keeper, pp. 130-131.

79. Though it was still being hunted in Germany,
Austria, Spain and Russia, the wild boar had become extinct
in England in Plantagenet times, and Charles I's effort to
restock them in the New Forest had been a failure. Whole
roast pig was still being served as a top or bottom dish;
for recipes see above pp. 82-83.

tied up to preserve its shape, it could be boiled, roasted

or baked and served with a ragout and garnishes--sippets,

fried forcemeat balls, sweetbreads, oysters, bacon, hard-

cooked egg yolks, lemon and orange slices, barberries,

truffles, artichoke bottoms.[80] Mrs. Glasse recommended

an extra touch: "You must bake the tongue with the head,

and don't cut it out. It will lie the handsomer in the

dish."[81] Or it could be baked the Dutch way, surrounded

by rice and Spanish peas.[82]

The "best way" was to halve it and use part of the

meat in the ragout:

> To hash a calf's head.
>
> Boil the head almost enough, then take the
> best half and with a sharp knife take it nicely
> from the bone, with the two eyes. Lay it in a
> little deep dish before a good fire, and take
> care no ashes fall into it, and then hack it
> with a knife cross and cross: grate some nut-
> meg all over, a very little pepper and salt, a
> few sweet herbs, some crumbs of bread, and a
> little lemon-peel chopped very fine; baste it
> with a little butter, then baste it again and
> pour over it the yolks of two eggs; keep the
> dish turning that it may be all brown alike:
> cut the other half and tongue into little thin
> bits, and set on a pint of drawn gravy in a
> sauce-pan, a little bundle of sweet herbs, an
> onion, a little pepper and salt, a glass of

---

80. Smith, Compleat Housewife, p. 30; Glasse, Art of Cookery, pp. 27-28, ɔ2, 57; Raffald, English House-keeper, p. 87.

81. Glasse, Art of Cookery, p. 28.

82. Ibid., p. 371.

red wine, and two shalots; boil all these together a few minutes, then strain it through
a sieve, and put it into a clean stew-pan with
the hash. Flour the meat before you put it in,
and put in a few mushrooms, a spoonful of the
pickle, two spoonfuls of catchup, and a few
truffles and morels; stir all these together
for a few minutes, then beat up half the brains
and stir into the stew-pan, and a little piece
of butter rolled in flour. Take the other half
of the brains and beat them up with a little
lemon-peel cut fine, a little nutmeg grated, a
little beaten mace, a little thyme shred small,
a little parsley, the yolk of an egg, and have
some good dripping boiling in a stew-pan; then
fry the brains in little cakes, about as big
as a crown-piece. Fry about twenty oysters
dipped in the yolk of an egg, toast some slices
of bacon, fry a few force-meat balls, and have
ready a hot dish; if pewter, over a few clear
coals; if china, over a pan of hot water. Pour
in your hash, then lay in your toasted head,
throw the force-meat balls over the hash, and
garnish the dish with fried oysters, the fried
brains, and lemon; throw the rest over the
hash, lay the bacon round the dish, and send
it to table.[83]

Dressed as a mock turtle it was even more elaborate.

The ears received special attention because they made

what was called "the crown of the turtle": stuffed with

forcemeat and tied with cloths to keep them erect during

the final stewing, they were arranged on the serving

platter so that the tops met around a large forcemeat

---

83. Ibid., pp. 26-27; cf. Harrison, Pocket-book,
pp. 25-26, 32-33. A simple hash was relatively appetizing,
or a calf's head might be collared and served cold, sliced,
as a side dish. Smith, Compleat Housewife, pp. 12, 14;
Raffald, English House-keeper, pp. 85-89.

ball set between them.[84]

A comparable extravagance suitable for the bottom of the table was called "a porcupine," which could be made of breast of veal or flat ribs of beef. Boned, rolled with an elaborate forcemeat, and skewered firmly, it was then larded in parallel rows across the top with strips of bacon, sliced ham or tongue, sliced cucumbers and lemon peel, then baked and served with the usual gravy sauce and garnishes.[85]

Similar "disguises" recommended for the top or bottom of a large table were made from large cuts: a leg of veal, lamb or mutton,[86] a shoulder of veal or mutton,[87] a saddle of mutton,[88] or a boned rump of beef.[89] Special decorations could be as original as one could wish: a sprig of myrtle in a fish's mouth, for example, or the tail feathers of a pheasant stuck in the tail of the roasted bird before serving it.[90]

---

84. Raffald, English House-keeper, pp. 82-83; cf. Harrison, Pocket-book, p. 47, serving it in a turtle shell.

85. Ibid., pp. 89-90, 116.

86. Ibid., pp. 101-102; Glasse, Art of Cookery, pp. 31, 44; Smith, Compleat Housewife, p. 22.

87. Glasse, Art of Cookery, pp. 45, 55-57; Raffald, English House-keeper, p. 104.

88. Glasse, Art of Cookery, pp. 45-46.

89. Ibid., p. 35.

90. Raffald, English House-keeper, pp. 29, 65.

Small side dishes were often composed of one of the
supplementary ingredients of more elaborate made dishes,
served in similar sauces--fowl livers, ox palates, sweetbreads, cocks' combs, pigs' ears or pettitoes, oysters,
eels, cod sounds--sometimes forced, or simply fricasseed
or ragouted.[91] Vegetables also were dressed separately
in fricassee or ragout--artichoke bottoms, onions, asparagus, cauliflower, cabbage, cucumbers, beans, peas, turnips, carrots, mushrooms--and cabbage and cucumbers were
sometimes forced.[92]

For the second course or for a supper, a cold mixture in high favor was the Salmagundi. Mrs. Randolph
directed:

> Turn a bowl on the dish, and put on it in
> regular rings, beginning at the bottom, the
> following ingredients, all minced:--anchovies
> with the bones taken out, the white meat of
> fowls without the skin, hard boiled eggs, the
> yelks and whites chopped separately, parsley,
> the lean of old ham scraped, the inner stalks
> of celery; put a row of capers round the bottom
> of the bowl, and dispose the others in a fanci-
> ful manner; put a little pyramid of butter on
> the top, and have a small glass with egg mixed
> as for sallad, to eat with the salmagundi.[93]

---

91. Smith, Compleat Housewife, p. 11; Glasse, Art
of Cookery, pp. 47, 57-58, 107-112; Raffald, English
House-keeper, p. 30.

92. Smith, Compleat Housewife, p. 28; Glasse, Art of
Cookery, pp. 109-113; Randolph, Virginia Housewife, p. 106.

93. Randolph, Virginia Housewife, p. 153.

Mrs. Raffald used pickled herrings instead of anchovies, shaped her butter like a pineapple, and decorated it with the bones of the herrings arranged "with the tails up to the butter, and the head...on the edge of the dish"; or, a second way, she substituted a large Seville orange for the upside-down bowl as a base and arranged her butter in little curls decorated with sprigs of parsley.[94]

Mrs. Glasse suggested that the Salmagundi be given top billing on the supper table as the middle dish. She placed the minced herring or anchovies in "the top plate in the middle, which should stand higher than the rest," and in "the other plates round" an assortment of "just what you fancy"--thinly sliced cucumbers, perhaps, and chopped apple, onion, egg whites, egg yolks, celery, pickled gherkins, pickled red cabbage--then decorated generously with water cress and nasturtium flowers and served with oil and vinegar dressing alongside.[95]

A true green salad, in modern taste, was offered by Mrs. Randolph:

TO DRESS SALAD.

To have this delicate dish in perfection,
the lettuce, pepper grass, chervil, cress, &c.
should be gathered early in the morning, nicely

---

94. Raffald, English House-keeper, pp. 280-281.

95. Glasse, Art of Cookery, pp. 163-164. Cf. Harrison, Pocket-book, pp. 26, 91, using cold veal or turkey

picked, washed, and laid in cold water, which
will be improved by adding ice; just before dinner is ready to be served, drain the water from
your salad, cut it into a bowl, giving the proper proportions of each plant; prepare the following mixture to pour over it: boil two fresh
eggs ten minutes, put them in water to cool,
then take the yelks in a soup plate, pour on
them a table spoonful of cold water, rub them
with a wooden spoon until they are perfectly
dissolved; then add two spoonsful of oil: when
well mixed, put in a teaspoonful of salt, one
of powdered sugar, and one of made mustard;
when all these are united and quite smooth, stir
in two table spoonsful of common, and two of
tarragon vinegar; put it over the salad, and
garnish the top with the whites of the eggs cut
into rings, and lay around the edge of the bowl
young scallions, they being the most delicate
of the onion tribe.[96]

Sweet dishes suitable for the second course included

the fruit pies and tarts, cakes and puddings already de-

scribed. For ball suppers, dessert jellies were much in

favor and very elegant when served in special glasses,

which could be arranged on glass plates to form a pyramid.[97]

---

and a similar assortment of seafood and vegetables; also
Bradley, British Housewife, pp. 360-361, using a shredded
lettuce base.

96. Randolph, Virginia Housewife, pp. 95-96; cf.
John Evelyn, Acetaria, A Discourse of Sallets (1st edn.
1699, reprint Brooklyn Botanic Garden, 1937).

97. Virginia houses were sometimes equipped with
glass pyramids--Green Spring, for one. See the appraisal
of the estate, 1767, in Ludwell Papers, Virginia Historical
Society, printed in part in Virginia Magazine of History
and Biography, XXI (1913), p. 410. Governor Fauquier owned
several. York County Records, Book XXII, Wills and Inventories, 83-90.

There were several congealing agents available.

Isinglass was the purest form of gelatine known at that

time. Hartshorn shavings could be used, but most cooks

found that calves' feet produced better consistency and

flavor if the proper care was taken in the preparation.

Mrs. Randolph's directions were explicit and reliable:

TO MAKE JELLY FROM FEET.

Boil four calfs' feet, that have been nicely cleaned, and the hoofs taken off; when the
feet are boiled to pieces, strain the liquor
through a colander, and when cold, take all the
grease off, and put the jelly in a skillet,
leaving the dregs which will be at the bottom.
There should be from four feet, about two quarts
of jelly: pour into it one quart of white wine,
the juice of six fresh lemons strained from the
seeds, one pound and a half of powdered loaf
sugar, a little pounded cinnamon and mace, and
the rind thinly pared from two of the lemons;
wash eight eggs very clean, whip up the whites
to a froth, crush the shells and put with them,
mix it with the jelly, set it on the fire, stir
it occasionally till the jelly is melted, but
do not touch it afterwards. When it has boiled
till it looks quite clear on one side, and the
dross accumulates on the other, take off carefully the thickest part of the dross, and pour
the jelly in the bag; put back what runs through,
until it becomes quite transparent--then set a
pitcher under the bag, and put a cover all over
to keep out the dust: the jelly looks much
prettier when it is broken to fill the glasses.
The bag should be made of cotton or linen, and
be suspended in a frame made for the purpose.
The feet of hogs make the palest coloured jelly;
those of sheep are a beautiful amber-colour,
when prepared.[98]

---

98. Randolph, Virginia Housewife, pp. 116-117. Cf.
Glasse, Art of Cookery, p. 286; Harrison, Pocket-book, pp.
145, 148-149; Raffald, English House-keeper, pp. 191-192;

Instead of being served in glasses, the jelly could be set in molds and served, unmolded, on plates. Fluted tin molds in a variety of popular shapes were available in Virginia shops, including melons, hedgehogs, stars, half-moons, sunflowers, obelisks, steeples, swans, fish, eggs, hens and chickens, packs of cards.[99] These molds were used also for blancmange and flummery. At that time blancmange was a very delicate jelly made opaque by the addition of almond paste. Jefferson's Paris recipe called for a paste of sweet and bitter almonds "liquified" with cream and sweetened with sugar, then added to isinglass dissolved in boiling water and strained through a napkin.[100] Mrs. Randolph used milk instead of cream:

> Break one ounce of isinglass into very small pieces; wash it well, and pour on a pint of boiling water; next morning, add a quart of milk, boil it till the isinglass is dissolved, strain it, put in two ounces sweet almonds, blanched and pounded; sweeten it, and put it in the mould--when stiff, turn them into a deep dish, and put raspberry cream around them. For a change, stick thin slips of blanched almonds all over the blanc mange, and dress round with syllabub, nicely frothed.[101]

Bradley, British Housewife, pp. 195-196.

99. The following advertisements are typical: John Carter, Virginia Gazette (Purdie and Dixon), June 25, 1767; Sarah Pitt, ibid., December 14, 1769; Balfour and Barroud, ibid., July 25, 1766.

100. Kimball, Jefferson's Cook Book, p. 14; cf. Carême's recipe in Larousse Gastronomique, p. 150.

101. Randolph, Virginia Housewife, pp. 150-151.

The syllabub which dressed this dish was also a popular dessert served alone in syllabub glasses. Its basic ingredients were white wine and cream, which were sweetened and whipped for half an hour. As the froth formed, it was carefully taken off by spoonfuls and placed on a hair sieve to drain. When froth no longer rose, the clear mixture remaining in the bowl was poured into glasses and the mounds of froth placed on top as "high" as possible. A mixture of several kinds of wine might be used--Rhenish and sack, for example--and lemon or orange juice was often added to the wine. If special glasses were not used, the syllabub could be served in jelly glasses or china dishes.[102]

Flummery, also opaque, was less delicate than blancmange but easier to prepare:

> One measure of jelly, one of cream, and half a one of wine; boil it fifteen minutes over a slow fire, stirring all the time; sweeten it, and add a spoonful of orange flower or rose water; cool it in a mould, turn it in a dish, and pour around it cream, seasoned in any way you like.[103]

Mrs. Glasse served her flummery "either with wine or cream."[104]

A molded jelly, blancmange or flummery was often

---

102. Ibid., p. 148; Smith, Compleat Housewife, pp. 89, 97; Glasse, Art of Cookery, p. 284; Raffald, English House-keeper, pp. 207-208; Harrison, Pocket-book, p. 151.

103. Randolph, Virginia Housewife, p. 119.

104. Glasse, Art of Cookery, pp. 187, 189.

tinted "the natural colour of what it represents": for green, spinach juice was added; for blue, syrup of violets; for yellow, either egg yolks or saffron water; for red, cochineal or alkanet root pounded and dissolved in brandy; for brown, chocolate; for white, cream.[105] With the use of molds and coloring a variety of "pretty decorations for a grand table" was possible; for example, Mrs. Raffald's

HEN and CHICKENS in JELLY.

Make some flummery with a deal of sweet almonds in it, colour a little of it brown with chocolate, and put it in a mould the shape of a hen; then colour some more flummery, with the yolk of a hard egg beat as fine as possible, leave part of your flummery white; then fill the moulds of seven chickens, three with white flummery, and three with yellow, and one the colour of the hen; when they are cold turn them into a deep dish, put under, and round them, lemon peel boiled tender and cut like straw, then put a little clear calf's foot jelly under them, to keep them in their places, and let it stand till it is stiff, then fill up your dish with more jelly.[106]

In the same way, a half-moon and stars of blancmange or clear jelly could be held in place in a sky of lemon cream or flummery tinted with cochineal and chocolate.[107]

---

105. Randolph, Virginia Housewife, p. 151; Harrison, Pocket-book, p. 146; Glasse, Art of Cookery, pp. 217, 286; Raffald, English House-keeper, pp. 194, 198, 204; Bradley, British Housewife, pp. 196-197; Custis, Booke of Sweetmeats, No. 165.

106. Raffald, English House-keeper, pp. 198-199.

107. Ibid.; Glasse, Art of Cookery, pp. 289-290;

Fish molds could be used in a similar arrangement called a Fish Pond. Flummery fish of different sizes were first molded, then unmolded and placed a few at a time in progressive layers of clear jelly in a shallow bowl; each layer was allowed to set before another was poured in so that the fish would "keep their places." When the bowl of jelly was unmolded and inverted on a plate, the opaque fish appeared to be swimming about at different levels in the pond.[108]

Card molds required added attention for a realistic effect:

> To make CRIBBAGE CARDS in FLUMMERY.
>
> Fill five square tins the size of a card with very stiff flummery, when you turn them out have ready a little cochineal dissolved in brandy, and strain it through a muslin rag, then take a camel's hair pencil, and make hearts and diamonds with your cochineal, then rub a little chocolate with a little eating oil upon a marble slab till it is very fine and bright, then make clubs and spades; pour a little Lisbon wine into the dish, and send it up.[109]

If the housewife had no jelly molds she could still prepare elaborate desserts, a Hen's Nest, for example:

> Get five small eggs, make a hole at one

Bradley, _British Housewife_, pp. 363-365.

108. Raffald, _English House-keeper_, p. 194. For something very elaborate, see her recipe, p. 198, for "GILDED FISH in JELLY," in which blancmange fish were gilded with gold leaf before being set to swim in jelly or Lisbon wine.

109. _Ibid._, p. 205.

end, and empty the shells--fill them with
blanc mange: when stiff and cold, take off
the shells, pare the yellow rind very thin
from six lemons, boil them in water till tender, then cut them in thin strips to resemble
straw, and preserve them with sugar; fill a
small deep dish half full of nice jelly--when
it is set, put the straw on in form of a nest,
and lay the eggs in it. It is a beautiful
dish for a dessert or supper.[110]

Or a Hedge Hog:

Take two pounds of blanched almonds, beat
them well in a mortar, with a little canary
and orange-flower water, to keep them from oil-
ing. Make them into stiff paste, then beat in
the yolks of twelve eggs, leave out five of the
whites, put to it a pint of cream, sweetened
with sugar, put in half a pound of sweet butter
melted, set it on a furnace or slow fire, and
keep it constantly stirring, till it is stiff
enough to be made in the form of a hedge-hog,
then put it into a dish, take a pint of cream
and the yolks of four eggs beat up, sweetened
with sugar to your palate. Stir them together
over a slow fire till it is quite hot, then
pour it round the hedge-hog in a dish, and let
it stand till it is cold, and serve it up. Or
a rich calf's foot jelly made clear and good,
and pour it into the dish round the hedge-hog;
and when it is cold, it looks pretty, and
makes a pretty dish: or it looks pretty in
the middle of a table for supper.[111]

A clear jelly with fruit molded in it could be

attractive, as suggested by Mrs. Raffald:

Put half a pint of clear stiff calf's foot
jelly into a bason, when it is set and stiff,
lay in three fine ripe peaches, and a bunch

---

110. Randolph, Virginia Housewife, p. 151; cf. Raffald, English House-keeper, p. 195.

111. Glasse, Art of Cookery, p. 288.

of grapes with the stalks up, put a few vine
leaves over them, then fill up your bowl with
jelly, and let it stand till the next day;
then set your bason to the brim in hot water,
and as soon as you find it leaves the bason,
lay your dish over it, and turn your jelly
carefully upon it: garnish with flowers.[112]

To balance jelled desserts in a formal table set-

ting, various creams and custards were popular. To make

a fine cream:

Take a pint of cream, sweeten it to your
palate, grate a little nutmeg, put in a spoonful of orange-flower water and rose-water, and
two spoonfuls of sack, beat up four eggs, but
two whites; stir all together one way over the
fire till it is thick, have cups ready, and
pour it in.[113]

A custard was made in much the same way though usually with-

out egg whites, and the cups were often set in a pan of

water and baked briefly, as in modern custom. Creams

and custards that did not have to be reheated were poured

directly into glasses or china dishes which could be sent

to the table.

Thickening agents less appetizing than heavy cream

and eggs--rice, barley, or the sago imported from the

East Indies--produced creams similar to modern packaged

puddings. To prepare sago, Mrs. Harrison directed:

To every Ounce of Sago put a Pint and a

---

112. Raffald, English House-keeper, p. 197.

113. Glasse, Art of Cookery, p. 283.

Half of Water, pick your Sago clean, boil it
Half an Hour, and skim it clean; then put in
Lemons and fine Sugar, and a little Cinnamon,
to your Taste.[114]

Popular flavors included lemon and orange, peach and

apricot, plum and quince, berry juices, chocolate, coffee,

tea, almond, pistachio.[115] Though creams and custards

could not be molded without adding jelly to them, there

were several conventional dishes similar to elaborate

molded jellies:

TO MAKE A TRIFLE.

Put slices of Savoy cake or Naples biscuit
at the bottom of a deep dish; wet it with white
wine, and fill the dish nearly to the top with
rich boiled custard; season half a pint of
cream with white wine and sugar; whip it to a
froth--as it rises, take it lightly off, and
lay it on the custard; pile it up high and
tastily--decorate it with preserves of any kind,
cut so thin as not to bear the froth down by
its weight.[116]

Macaroons could be substituted for the Savoy cakes or Naples

biscuit, and some recipes preferred sherry to other wines.

When the lining of cake was omitted and the custard was

---

114. Harrison, Pocket-book, p. 195. See also Smith,
Compleat Housewife, pp. 161, 163; Glasse, Art of Cookery,
pp. 282, 361; Bradley, British Housewife, pp. 262, 699-700;
Randolph, Virginia Housewife, p. 149.

115. Smith, Compleat Housewife, pp. 54, 84-95;
Glasse, Art of Cookery, pp. 280-283, 357, 362-363; Raffald,
English House-keeper, pp. 248-258; Randolph, Virginia
Housewife, pp. 119, 148-149; Bradley, British Housewife,
pp. 261-263, 362-363.

116. Randolph, Virginia Housewife, p. 147.

flavored with berry juices, the dish was called a Fool.[117]

There were floating islands of various sorts; Mrs.

Glasse made it this way:

> You may take a soop-dish, according to
> the size and quantity you would make, but a
> pretty deep glass dish is best, and set it on
> a china dish; first take a quart of the thick-
> est cream you can get, make it pretty sweet
> with fine sugar, pour in a gill of sack, grate
> the yellow rhind of a lemon in, and mill the
> cream till it is all of a thick froth, then as
> carefully as you can pour the thin from the
> froth into a dish; take a French roll, or as
> many as you want, cut it as thin as you can,
> lay a layer of that as light as possible on
> the cream, then a layer of currant jelly, then
> a very thin layer of roll, and then hartshorn
> jelly, then French roll, and over that whip
> your froth which you saved off the cream very
> well milled up, and lay at top as high as you
> can heap it; and as for the rim of the dish,
> set it round with fruit or sweetmeats, accord-
> ing to your fancy. This looks very pretty in
> the middle of a table with candles round it,
> and you may make it of as many different col-
> ours as you fancy, and according to what jel-
> lies and giams or sweet-meats you have; or at
> the bottom of your dish you may put the thick-
> est cream you can get: but this is as you fancy.[118]

By the end of the century ice cream was being made

in fruit and berry flavors and with vanilla, chocolate,

---

117. Glasse, Art of Cookery, pp. 153, 285; Harrison,
Pocket-book, pp. 152-153; Raffald, English House-keeper,
p. 255; Bradley, British Housewife, p. 199; Custis, Booke
of Cookery, No. 109.

118. Glasse, Art of Cookery, p. 290. Cf. Randolph,
Virginia Housewife, pp. 147-148; Raffald, English House-
keeper, pp. 200, 258; Bradley, British Housewife, pp. 365-366.

coffee, almonds and black walnuts.[119] Mrs. Raffald's

recipe did not require a freezer:

To make ICE CREAM.

Pare, stone, and scald twelve ripe apricots, beat them fine in a marble mortar, put
to them six ounces of double refined sugar, a
pint of scalding cream, work it through a hair
sieve, put it into a tin that has a close cover,
set it in a tub of ice broken small, and a
large quantity of salt put amongst it, when you
see your cream grow thick around the edges of
your tin, stir it, and set it in again till it
grows quite thick, when your cream is all froze
up, take it out of your tin, and put it into
the mould you intend it to be turned out of,
then put on the lid, and have ready another tub
with ice and salt in as before, put your mould
in the middle, and lay your ice under and over
it, let it stand four or five hours, dip your
tin in warm water when you turn it out; if it
be summer, you must not turn it out till the
moment you want it; you may use any sort of
fruit if you have not apricots, only observe
to work it fine.[120]

Mrs. Glasse recommended the use of a freezer pur-

chased from a pewterer:

To make ice cream.

Take two pewter basons, one larger than
the other; the inward one must have a close
cover, into which you are to put your cream,
and mix it with raspberries, or whatever you
like best, to give it a flavour and a colour.
Sweeten it to your palate; then cover it close,
and set it into the larger bason. Fill it
with ice, and a handful of salt: let it stand
in this ice three quarters of an hour, then un-
cover it, and stir the cream well together;

---

119. Randolph, Virginia Housewife, pp. 142-146;
Glasse, Art of Cookery, p. 332.

120. Raffald, English House-keeper, pp. 249-250.

cover it close again, and let it stand half an hour longer, after that turn it into your plate. These things are made at the pewterers.[121]

Mrs. Randolph explained just how the freezer should be made and used:

OBSERVATIONS ON ICE CREAMS.

It is the practice with some indolent cooks, to set the freezer containing the cream, in a tub with ice and salt, and put it in the ice house; it will certainly freeze there; but not until the watery particles have subsided, and by the separation destroyed the cream. A freezer should be twelve or fourteen inches deep, and eight or ten wide. This facilitates the operation very much, by giving a larger surface for the ice to form, which it always does on the sides of the vessel; a silver spoon with a long handle should be provided for scraping the ice from the sides as soon as formed; and when the whole is congealed, pack it in moulds (which must be placed with care, lest they should not be upright,) in ice and salt, till sufficiently hard to retain the shape--they should not be turned out till the moment they are to be served. The freezing tub must be wide enough to leave a margin of four or five inches all around the freezer, when placed in the middle--which must be filled up with small lumps of ice mixed with salt--a larger tub would waste the ice. The freezer must be kept constantly in motion during the process, and ought to be made of pewter, which is less liable than tin to be worn in holes, and spoil the cream by admitting the salt water.[122]

Her recipes for the cream mixture were characteristically practical. Rich cream was preferred as the base, but a boiled custard might be substituted "when cream cannot be

---

121. Glasse, <u>Art of Cookery</u>, p. 332.

122. Randolph, <u>Virginia Housewife</u>, pp. 142-143.

had," and the mixture should be made "very sweet, for much

of the sugar is lost in the operation of freezing." Fi-

nally, she stated the current rule for serving the dessert:

"When ice creams are not put into shapes, they should always

be served in glasses with handles"--i.e., conventional jelly

or syllabub glasses.[123] She also made sherbets:

LEMONADE ICED.
Make a quart of rich lemonade, whip the
whites of six fresh eggs to a strong froth--
mix them well with the lemonade, and freeze it.
The juice of morello cherries, or of currants
mixed with water and sugar, and prepared in
the same way, make very delicate ices.[124]

Mrs. Randolph's detailed instructions suggest that

ice cream was still something of a rarity when she wrote

her cookbook. The question of who was the first Virginian

to serve it is variously answered. While Dolley Madison

usually gets the credit, there are earlier examples of the

ownership of freezers and, of course, it may have been

made as Mrs. Raffald directed before anyone purchased a

freezer. Washington bought one in May of 1784, shortly

after his return to Mount Vernon, when he was building a

greenhouse and improving his icehouse.[125] That same year

Jefferson in Paris copied out a recipe using custard and

---

123. Ibid., pp. 143, 144.

124. Ibid., p. 146.

125. Kimball, Jefferson's Cook Book, p. 2, cites
the purchase.

vanilla flavoring and requiring that it be frozen in a sor-
betière and molded in the manner described in the English

cookbooks. Presumably he brought home a French freezer to

go with the recipe.[126] Another Virginian, Theodorick Bland,

in 1786 asked his brother-in-law St. George Tucker to have

a pewter one made for him in New York or Philadelphia;

while he furnished a crude drawing of the "Salbotiore" he

preferred ("an obtuse Cone with a top fitted to it"), he

suggested that Tucker consult some of the "French Gentlemen"

among their friends for an exact "pattern for it."[127] At

the end of the century another member of the Williamsburg

circle, a friend of Tucker and of Jefferson, Anne Blair

Banister, on a round of visits in the Northern Neck com-

plained: "I made myself sick with Ice creams water melons

Plumbs &c.... alas! so much frigidity does not suit us old

folks."[128]

---

126. Ibid., pp. 2-3. At least one Virginian had
enjoyed it earlier. William Black, traveling with the
Virginia commissioners for the Lancaster Treaty with the
Iroquois in 1744, stopped off in Annapolis; there Governor Thomas Bladen, whose wife was a Frenchwoman, enter-
tained them in a splendid manner. Among the "Rarities"
served at dinner was "some fine Ice Cream." R. A. Brock, ed.,
"Journal of William Black, 1744," Pennsylvania Magazine of
History and Biography, I (1877), 126.

127. Bland to Tucker, August 14, 1786, Tucker-Coleman Papers, College of William and Mary. CW M-1021-5.

128. Anne Banister to [Betsey Whiting], August 16,
1799, in Frederick Horner, History of the Blair, Banister,
and Braxton Families... (Philadelphia, 1898), pp. 104-106.

VII. FOOD PRESERVATION

With refrigeration and canning yet unknown, the colonial housewife depended upon other expedients to keep
her food supplies edible. Meat, the most important ele-
ment in the Virginia diet, posed special problems because
it spoiled quickly in the warm climate. The practice of
preserving it with salt was so universal that guests in
private homes and public taverns found salted meat on the
menu at nearly every meal. One of Rochambeau's soldiers,
for example, Lieutenant Robertnier, observed that Virginians ate a great deal of it because "the heat in summer
is such that...fresh meat must be eaten within 24 hours;
after that, the meat is spoiled."[1] Hogs, which furnished
"the principal food of the inhabitants," were never

---

1. He attributed the "bad teeth" characteristic of
men and women throughout the colony to the salted meat
diet. Louis Jean Baptiste Silvestre de Robertnier, Journal
des guerre faites en Amerique pendans les années, 1780,
1781, 1782, 1783 avec quelques dissertations sur les moeurs
& coutumes des américains..., Rhode Island Historical Society; typescript translated by Prof. Edouard R. Massey, pp.
156-159. CW M-71. Cf. Dr. George Gilmer's theory of the
relationship between physical disorders of all kinds and
the consumption of salt meat, in a speech to the inhabitants of Albemarle, [1775], "Papers of George Gilmer, of
'Pen Park'," ed. by R. A. Brock, Virginia Historical Society Collections (Richmond, 1887), pp. 119-120.

slaughtered in summer, and pork was seldom eaten fresh.[2]

"They have a particular way to prepare, salt, and smoke it," Robertnier explained, and "although they use almost the same processes as in France, ours cannot be compared to the quality and taste of theirs."[3]

Hog-killing time came in the late fall, with the first cold weather and after the hogs had been fattened in the woods on mast (acorns, chestnuts, and the like) or in a pen on corn. Mrs. Randolph provided detailed instructions for the treatment of all parts of the freshly slaughtered hogs:

> ...To secure them against the possibility of spoiling, salt them before they get cold; take out the chine or back-bone from the neck to the tail, cut the hams, shoulders and middlings; take the ribs from the shoulders and the leaf fat from the hams: ...rub a large table spoonful of saltpetre on the inside of each ham, for some minutes, then rub both sides well with salt, sprinkle the bottom of the tub with salt, lay the hams with the skin downward, and put a good deal of salt between each layer; salt the shoulders and middlings in the same manner, but less saltpetre is necessary; cut the jowl or chop from the head, and rub it with salt and saltpetre. You should cut off the feet just above the knee joint; take off the ears and nose, and lay them in a large tub of cold water for souse.

---

2. Robertnier, Journal, p. 160. Dr. Lewis Beebe noted the same custom in Maryland: "Their pork is all converted to Bacon--This article is upon the table every day the year round." Journal, II, February 28, 1800, Historical Society of Pennsylvania. CW M-65.

3. Robertnier, Journal, pp. 166-167.

When the jowls have been in salt two weeks,
hang them up to smoke--do so with the shoulders and middlings at the end of three weeks,
and the hams at the end of four. If they remain longer in salt they will be hard. Remem-
ber to hang the hams and shoulders with the
hocks down, to preserve the juices. Make a
good smoke every morning, and be careful not
to have a blaze; the smoke-house should stand
alone, for any additional heat will spoil the
meat. During the hot weather, beginning the
first of April, it should be occasionally
taken down, examined--rubbed with hickory
ashes, and hung up again.[4]

This was the standard curing process for home use

and also for sale, principally in the West Indies. Some

householders added brown sugar to the salt and saltpetre,

others omitted the saltpetre and used hickory ash in the

first rubbing[5]--probably an expedient learned from the

Virginia Indians, who had no salt and seasoned their food

with salt ash.[6] Getting good salt was a continuing pro-

blem in the colony. Since attempts to produce it from

---

4. Mary Randolph, The Virginia Housewife...(Philadelphia, 1855), p. 48. Cf. the English method described
in E. Smith, The Compleat Housewife...(Williamsburg,
1742), pp. 25-26; Sarah Harrison, The House-keeper's
Pocket-book...(6th edn., London, 1755), pp. 134-136;
[Hannah Glasse], The Art of Cookery...(7th edn., London,
1760), pp. 256-259; Elizabeth Raffald, The Experienced
English House-keeper...(4th edn., London, 1775), pp.
306-308.

5. Nicholas Cresswell, The Journal of Nicholas
Cresswell, 1774-1777 (New York, 1924), p. 199.

6. Robert Beverley, The History and Present State
of Virginia, ed. by Louis B. Wright (Chapel Hill, 1947),
p. 180.

Chesapeake waters always failed because of low salinity,

all kinds had to be imported, and from British merchants.[7]

Though all salt in use at that time was made from sea water,

there were distinctions in quality due to the properties of

the water and the method of evaporation. Liverpool salt

was good for table use but inadequate for curing meat or

fish; for this purpose the superior Lisbon salt was re-

quired.[8]

Either in summer or early fall Virginians cured

large cuts of fresh beef for winter use, following the

English procedure in this case. Each piece was thoroughly

salted and placed fleshy side down in the salting tubs,

with extra salt above and below it. After ten days they

were all removed from the tubs and immersed in brine pre-

pared

> ...after the following manner: get a thirty
> gallon cask, take out one head, drive in the
> bung, and put some pitch on it, to prevent
> leaking. See that the cask is quite tight
> and clean. Put into it one pound of saltpetre

---

7. For brief descriptions of the critical shortage
during the Revolution see Gilmer's Albemarle speech and
David J. Mays, Edmund Pendleton, 1721-1803, A Biography
(Cambridge, 1952), II, 48-50.

8. Washington to John Murray and Company, March 8,
1786, in The Writings of George Washington..., ed. by John
C. Fitzpatrick (Washington, 1931-44), XXVIII, 389-390.
Recipes made a similar distinction between common salt
(British) and bay salt (from Southern Europe, preferably
the waters of the Bay of Biscay).

powdered, fifteen quarts of salt, and fifteen
gallons of cold water, stir it frequently,
until dissolved, throw over the cask a thick
cloth, to keep out the dust; look at it often
and take off the scum. These proportions have
been accurately ascertained.... This brine
...requires nothing more to be done to it except occasionally skimming the dross that rises.
It must be kept in a cool, dry place.... In
about ten days it will look red and be fit for
the table, but it will be red much sooner when
the brine becomes older.[9]

To "dry" beef for summer use, early in the spring

the same procedure was followed until the meat had been

in the brine for three weeks. At that time each piece

was taken out, wiped quite dry, and rubbed over with bran,

then hung in a cool, dry, dark place. During the summer

it was necessary to "look them over occasionally, and

after a long wet season, to lay them in the sun a few

hours."[10]

When a beef was killed in mid-summer, parts of it

might be preserved for use the next week:

TO CORN BEEF IN HOT WEATHER.
Take a piece of thin brisket or plate, cut
out the ribs nicely, rub it on both sides well
with two large spoonsful of pounded saltpetre;
pour on it a gill of molasses and a quart of

---

9. Randolph, Virginia Housewife, pp. 22-24. Cf.
Smith, Compleat Housewife, pp. 26-27; Glasse, Art of
Cookery, pp. 271, 382; Raffald, English House-keeper, p.
308.

10. Ibid., p. 24.

salt; rub them both in; put it in a vessel just
large enough to hold it, but not tight, for the
bloody brine must run off as it makes, or the
meat will spoil. Let it be well covered, top,
bottom and sides, with the molasses and salt.
In four days you may boil it, tied up in a
cloth with the salt, &c. about it: when done,
take the skin off nicely, and serve it up.[11]

Settlers in the Shenandoah Valley and other frontier

communities sometimes followed the Indian method of dry-

ing meat without salt.[12] When Nicholas Cresswell and

his companions killed a buffalo bull in Kentucky, he re-

corded the jerking procedure:

[Thursday, May 18, 1775.] All hands employed
in curing our Buffalo meat, which is done in
a peculiar manner. The meat is first cut from
the bones in thin slices like beefsteaks, then
four forked sticks are stuck in the ground in
a square form, and small sticks laid on these
forks in the form of a gridiron about three
feet from the ground. The meat is laid on this
and a slow fire put under it, and turned until
it is done. This is called jerking the meat.
I believe it is an Indian method of preserving
meat. It answers very well, where salt is not
to be had, and will keep a long time if it be
secured from the wet. The lean parts eat very
dry. The Buffalo flesh differs little from
beef, only ranker taste.[13]

Small cuts of meat to be used as side dishes--pigs'

---

11. Ibid., pp. 25-26.

12. Inventories of estates in these areas occasionally list dried beef and venison of this kind. The Spanish all over Latin America used the same process, learned
from Peruvian Indians.

13. Cresswell, Journal, pp. 75-76. Cf. the De Bry
engraving of an Indian broiler for fish, reproduced in
Beverley, History, p. 179.

feet and ox palates, for example--were salted in brine like fresh beef, then pickled in spiced vinegar and stored in stone or glass jars, which did not absorb vinegar and salt.[14] Barrels or kegs were preferred for large quantities of oysters, which were easy to pickle because no brine was needed. Shucked and picked over for bits of shell, they were placed directly in a stewpan with some of their own liquor mixed with white wine or water, seasoned with salt, pepper and mace, stewed a few minutes, and poured into containers. When they had cooled, pale vinegar was added to the liquid--enough to give it "an agreeable acid."[15]

Other shellfish were pickled like oysters.[16] Recipes for salt fish were concerned with cooking the dried product rather than preserving the fresh fish. Apparently fish was seldom salted at home either in England or Virginia, though kegs of salt herring were often imported into the colony.[17]

---

14. Glasse, Art of Cookery, pp. 108, 269, 271.

15. Randolph, Virginia Housewife, p. 60.

16. Glasse, Art of Cookery, p. 269.

17. Fresh fish was available here the year round, but Mrs. Randolph gave a recipe for curing herring. For examples of imports see advertisements and notices in Virginia Gazette, passim, and of orders, Frances N. Mason, ed., John Norton & Sons Merchants of London and Virginia

Anything that could be "collared" could be preserved

in pickle. First the viand was boned and rolled tightly

about a forcemeat stuffing. Then it was securely bound

with a piece of broad tape and wrapped in a cloth for

stewing.[18] If it was not to be used at once, it was

drained, the cloth was removed, and the collar was kept

in a pickle of brine and vinegar until it was served in

thin round slices, garnished with herbs.[19] Mrs. Raffald

advised, "Make fresh pickle often, and your meat will

keep good a long time."[20]

In England to "souse" a turkey or a mackerel, tripe

or pigs' feet, was to pickle them in the same manner.[21]

In Virginia "to make souse" was to prepare pieces of fresh

pork in a special form not used for anything else. The

feet, ears and heads were scraped clean and soaked in

cold water until the blood was drawn off, then stewed in

salted meal gruel, boned, seasoned with salt, pepper and

(Richmond, 1937), pp. 19, 38, 57, 62, 66, 74, 137, 273.

18. See above pp. 44-45.

19. Smith, Compleat Housewife, pp. 17-19, 24-25; Harrison, Pocket-book, pp. 136-139; Glasse, Art of Cookery, pp. 30-31, 254-255; Raffald, English House-keeper, pp. 300-304.

20. Raffald, English House-keeper, p. 293.

21. Ibid., pp. 304-305; Glasse, Art of Cookery, pp. 230, 256.

nutmeg, and pressed into shapes to fit the storage pots.

Closely wrapped in a cloth, the souse was then immersed

in a brine of salted water and pale vinegar thickened with

a little fresh meal--"just enough to look white."[22]

Cooked meats could be preserved for future use in

earthenware pots sealed with butter. This process, called

potting, was recommended for all kinds of fowl, fish, and

seafood and for cuts of beef and venison.[23] Small fowl

or fish were baked whole, seasoned "according to your

palate, more or less," then cooled and drained of all

gravy and packed into pots as close together as possible.

The pot was sealed with clarified butter, carefully

poured in to fill all the crevices and to cover the vi-

ands "the thickness of a crown piece." The flavor of

wild fowl and bony fish was improved if they were boned

before baking. The meat of hares, larger fowls, eels,

lobsters and salmon was usually cooked in chunks and then

packed in the same way. Paper covers kept the pots free

from dust.[24]

---

22. Randolph, Virginia Housewife, pp. 50-51.

23. Mutton was not potted; in England it was generally available fresh, and in Virginia venison took its
place on the menu. Only pork sausage was potted; other
hog meat was cured with salt.

24. Smith, Compleat Housewife, pp. 19-20, 25, 28;
Harrison, Pocket-book, pp. 141-142; Glasse, Art of Cookery,

Cuts of beef were treated differently. After baking with the usual seasonings and plenty of butter, the meat was thoroughly drained and beaten in a mortar with fresh butter until it became "a fine paste." Then it was pressed down close in the pot, sealed with clarified butter, and stored in a cool, dry place. When it was finally used, it was cut out in slices and sent to the table garnished with curled parsley.[25]

Pork sausage, preferably fried in cakes or balls, could be potted in the same manner and sealed with melted lard instead of clarified butter. Packed raw into skins (i.e., gut cases) sausage kept equally well if hung in a dry place.[26]

Many vegetable products were made into pickle. The number and variety of recipes offered in each cookbook attest their importance as garnishes in winter menus. Artichokes, asparagus, beans, beets, cabbage and cauliflower were regularly pickled as well as the more common

---

pp. 230-232, 251-253, 259; Raffald, English House-keeper, pp. 293, 296-299.

25. Harrison, Pocket-book, pp. 139-141; Glasse, Art of Cookery, p. 252; Raffald, English House-keeper, pp. 293-296.

26. Smith, Compleat Housewife, p. 32; Harrison, Pocket-book, pp. 195-196; Glasse, Art of Cookery, pp. 250-251; Randolph, Virginia Housewife, p. 54.

cucumbers, mushrooms, and onions. The usual practice was to put the pieces or slices into hot brine and let them soak about ten days before draining them and transferring them to the cold pickle. The proper length of time to treat them with salt varied with different vegetables, according to the effect on their color and crispness. The basic pickle ingredient was vinegar, but verjuice or alegar or white wine was sometimes substituted and sugar was usually added. Popular pickling spices included red, black and white pepper, turmeric, mace, clove, nutmeg, ginger; also mustard seed, garlic, scraped horseradish, tarragon, dill, fennel, bay leaves.[27]

"Nice cooks" paid special attention to color. A hot vinegar mixture could be depended upon to preserve the green tint of gherkins and asparagus, or vine leaves could be placed in the pickle jar to augment the natural color. Some cooks recommended the use of copper pickling kettles to produce a brilliant green, though it was known that verdigris was poisonous.[28] For a good yellow pickle,

---

27. Smith, Compleat Housewife, pp. 37-43; Harrison, Pocket-book, pp. 167, 170-176; Glasse, Art of Cookery, pp. 262-271, 312; Raffald, English House-keeper, pp. 352-357; Randolph, Virginia Housewife, pp. 164-167, 169-170.

28. Smith, Compleat Housewife, pp. 39-40; Raffald, English House-keeper, p. 342.

things like sliced cucumbers were left in brine a longer
time, then drained and dried in the sun; the bleaching
and drying process made them absorb turmeric the better.[29]
Mushrooms and onions, which were preferred white, were
pickled in white wine, with white pepper the predominant
spice.[30] English walnuts were quite versatile: picked
before the shell began to harden, they could be pickled
either green or white; full-grown, they were made into
"black" walnut pickle.[31]

The best containers were stoneware jars "straight
from the bottom to the top, with stone covers to them"
and with very wide mouths so that the pickles could "be
taken out without breaking them."[32] Glass jars or wide-
mouthed bottles served equally well, though they were
more expensive because of breakage. If the jar was not
fitted with its own lid, it was sealed with oil, butter
or mutton fat and then covered with a piece of leather,
a bladder, or a coarse cloth folded several times and tied

---

29. Randolph, Virginia Housewife, pp. 166, 169.

30. Smith, Compleat Housewife, p. 42; Glasse, Art of Cookery, p. 312.

31. Glasse, Art of Cookery, pp. 260-262; Raffald, English House-keeper, pp. 347-349; Harrison, Pocket-book, pp. 169-170.

32. Randolph, Virginia Housewife, pp. 169-170.

194

on with tape. If the vegetable had a tendency to float

on the brine or vinegar, it was held under with a board

wrapped in a piece of flannel.[33]

There were other pickled delicacies, unknown today:

blossoms from sassafras and redbud trees, nasturtium

"buds"; herbs like parsley and samphire; barberries and

currants; pods from the "aerial" radish still cultivated

in Asia.[34] A few fruits were preserved in pickle--

presumably because they kept their color and shape better

than in syrup--mango melons, small green apples, peaches,

apricots, plums, and bunches of grapes. Lemon pickle

was useful also for seasoning sauces.[35]

Of the several kinds of catsup so important to sauces,

the most serviceable were mushroom and walnut. Mushrooms

were first chopped or crushed, salted generously and left

to stand overnight, then heated to extract the maximum

amount of juice; strained and blended with spices, the

---

33. Glasse, Art of Cookery, p. 268.

34. Smith, Compleat Housewife, pp. 38, 39, 41;
Glasse, Art of Cookery, pp. 264, 267-270; Raffald, English
House-keeper, pp. 346, 350-351; Randolph, Virginia House-
wife, pp. 167-168; John Clayton to Robert Boyle, An Account
of Virginia, Boyle Papers 39, Royal Society, film copy
American Philosophical Society, No. 5433, 5437.

35. Harrison, Pocket-book, pp. 176-180; Glasse, Art
of Cookery, pp. 263, 265-268; Randolph, Virginia Housewife,
pp. 161-162, 165, 169; Raffald, English House-keeper,
pp. 80-81, 344-345, 354.

mushroom liquor was simmered until reduced to half its
volume, cooled, and bottled. For walnut catsup, English
walnuts were gathered green and treated in much the same
way as mushrooms except that vinegar, red wine or alegar
was added to the walnut juice, and English cooks often
used anchovies and horseradish with the spices.[36]

Mrs. Randolph's recipe for tomato catsup was one of
the first to appear in print:

> Gather a peck of tomatos, pick out the
> stems, and wash them; put them on the fire with-
> out water, sprinkle on a few spoonsful of salt,
> let them boil steadily an hour, stirring them
> frequently; strain them through a colander, and
> then through a sieve; put the liquid on the fire
> with half a pint of chopped onions, half a quar-
> ter of an ounce of mace broke into small pieces;
> and if not sufficiently salt, add a little more--
> one table-spoonful of whole black pepper; boil
> all together until just enough to fill two bot-
> tles; cork it tight. Make it in August, in dry
> weather.[37]

Pleased with the flavor of tomato in soups and gravies,
she recommended two variations on the basic catsup. For
tomato marmalade, the fruit was gathered while quite green
and cooked until soft enough to put through a sieve; then
the pulp was added to the juice and stewed with pepper,
salt, cloves, and garlic until the mixture was thick. For

---

36. Smith, Compleat Housewife, p. 41; Harrison, Pocket-
book, pp. 170, 174; Glasse, Art of Cookery, pp. 308-309, 334;
Raffald, English House-keeper, pp. 338-339; Randolph, Virginia
Housewife, pp. 164, 169.

37. Randolph, Virginia Housewife, p. 162.

tomato soy, the ripe fruit was sliced and placed in a salting tub in layers with sliced onions between. After three days the mixture was stewed in a pickling kettle without additional liquid for about ten hours; then the juice was carefully strained off, seasoned with red and black pepper, cloves, and allspice, boiled "slowly and constantly during the whole of the day," cooled overnight and bottled the next day.[38]

Another novelty, oyster catsup, Mrs. Randolph prepared and used like mushroom catsup. Fresh oysters were crushed in a mortar with salt, red pepper and mace, then stewed briefly in white wine, strained, and bottled.[39]

Since the only produce market worthy of the name was in Norfolk, most housewives depended upon their own gardens for vegetables and fruits.[40] The earliest American book on kitchen gardening, written by John Randolph of Williamsburg, recorded his own experience in adapting

---

38. Ibid., pp. 162-163.

39. Ibid., pp. 94-95.

40. [Anne Ritson], A Poetical Picture of America... (London, 1809), lists products and prices in the Norfolk market of her day, about 1800. Robert Carter of Nomini Hall explained the situation: "Every Family here have small Farms which supplie them with Articles to be bought in good Markets. Such a Custom must inevitably bar every attempt towards improveing Markets." Carter to James Buchanan, May 10, 1764, in Robert Carter Letter Book, Colonial Williamsburg Archives.

English methods of vegetable growing to Virginia condi-

tions.[41] Presumably he incorporated in his manual things

learned from other Virginia gardeners, for he mentioned

some of them by name--Col. Thomas Turner of King George

County and Col. Philip Ludwell of James City, for example.

For these reasons his treatise may be accepted as a state-

ment of the best local practice.

By planting successive crops householders had many

of their favorite vegetables on their tables from spring

until late fall: French beans, kidney beans, limas, cu-

cumbers, cabbage, lettuce, peas, radishes, carrots, onions.

Fresh celery could be made available all the year. Spin-

ach sowed in July was ready in October and provided suc-

cessive cuttings until spring. By cutting off the tops of

some of his strawberries Randolph retarded their growth

and extended his strawberry season into the summer. With

a hotbed[42] he produced an early spring crop of cucumbers,

in his opinion "the most refreshing and delicate of all

vegetables." Other favorites--all seasonal--included ar-

tichokes, asparagus, broccoli, cauliflower, parsnips,

melons of several kinds, salsify and turnips.

---

41. [John Randolph], A Treatise on Gardening by a
Citizen of Virginia, ed. by Marjorie F. Warner (Richmond,
1924), probably written about 1760-1765.

42. There were garden glasses and greenhouses in
use in Virginia, but hotbeds were more common.

Randolph provided also specific instructions for winter storage in the tidewater climate. Cabbage was taken up by the roots in November and replanted under a ridge of earth with the heads to the south and the stems covered; thus protected they would keep all the winter. Cauliflower was placed in holes about two feet below the surface of the ground and covered with straw. Peas and kidney beans, still in their pods, were preserved in layers of salt. Root vegetables like carrots, potatoes and radishes were kept in layers of dry sand. Onion and garlic bulbs were taken up in July, dried and hung in "some room or garret, as close from air as possible."[43]

English custom offered a few other expedients to the thrifty housewife. Green peas, mushrooms, and artichoke bottoms partly cooked could be dried in the oven and bottled, then tightly corked or sealed with melted fat. Walnuts and lemons could be kept in large jars in layers of dry sand, or lemons could be hung "in a dry airy place" like herbs, on threads drawn through their hard nibs and knotted so as to keep them from touching each other.[44]

---

43. Randolph, _Treatise_, p. 35. The popular nineteenth-century convenience, the root cellar, was suited to less humid climates than that of the tidewater.

44. Smith, _Compleat Housewife_, p. 31; Glasse, _Art of Cookery_, pp. 309-311; Raffald, _English House-keeper_, pp. 358-362.

The bags of dried peas, beans and fruit sometimes entered in Virginia inventories suggest a limited use of the Indian method of drying them in the sun. Like jerked meat, these dried fruits and legumes were more common in the upcountry than in the humid tidewater.[45]

Confectionery was another art practiced by efficient housewives. It took several forms. Whole fruits or berries cooked and stored in syrup were called preserves. Mashed, they became marmalade, conserve, or jam. "Dried" (i.e., candied like modern crystallized fruit) they were confections or sweetmeats.[46] When their juices were mixed with syrup and reduced sufficiently to form hard candies, they were chips; when mashed pulp was used in the same way, they were called pastes. Strained juices were also used to make jelly, as in modern practice, and there were fruit and berry syrups. Brandied fruits were prepared by adding brandy to the syrup in which whole fruits were stored.

Mrs. Randolph's selection of recipes, reflecting Virginia tastes at the end of the century, emphasized

---

45. Beverley, History, p. 181; James Madison to his father, January 23, 1778, The Papers of James Madison, ed. by William T. Hutchinson and William M. E. Rachal (Chicago, 1962-), I, 222-223.

46. Distinctions were not precise. Sweetmeats was a general term for foods rich in sugar, as in Mrs. Custis's Booke of Sweetmeats, which included cakes and cookies as well as confections.

preserves--peaches, pears, quinces, cherries, strawberries, gooseberries, raspberries, and a sweet tomato marmalade. Her preserving kettle was made of bell metal,
"flat at the bottom, very large in diameter, but not
deep," with a tight-fitting cover and "handles at the
sides of the pan, for taking it off with ease when the
syrup boils too fast." Other desirable equipment included
a large chafing dish with long legs "for the convenience
of moving it to any part of the room," a ladle "the size
of a saucer, pierced and having a long handle" for "taking
up the fruit without syrup," small glasses or pots of a
maximum two-pound capacity, and "letter paper wet with
brandy" to cover the containers.[47]

The preserving process, properly managed, was a
tedious one:

> All delicate fruit should be done gently,
> and not allowed to remain more than half an
> hour after it begins to stew, before it is laid
> on dishes to cool; it must be put into the syrup
> again for the same time; continue this until it
> is sufficiently transparent. The advantage of
> this method is that the preserves are less lia-
> ble to boil to pieces, than when done all at one
> time. It is injudicious to put more in the pan
> at once, than can lie on the bottom without
> crowding.[48]

Not all fruits were preserved whole. Peaches were

---

47. Randolph, *Virginia Housewife*, pp. 154-155.

48. *Ibid.*, p. 155.

sometimes sliced or halved, quinces were cored and cherries stoned. But whatever the size of the fruits, care for appearance included attention to color as well as shape and transparency. Quinces, for example, were "light coloured if kept covered during the process, and red if the cover be taken off."[49]

For fruits "in brandy" the apricots, peaches or plums were gathered before they became completely ripe, and only those "free from blemish" were used. Bright red cherries with short stems were brandied in bunches. After the usual cooking and cooling, the fruits were placed in bottles one at a time, and then the bottles were filled with "equal quantities of syrup and French brandy."[50]

Mrs. Custis's Booke of Sweetmeats reflected the elegance and artificiality of tastes in Queen Anne's court. In addition to the conventional preserves,[51] she included the more elaborate confectionery that used flowers and herbs, roots and nuts as well as fruits and berries in a variety of crystallized preparations and hard candies to decorate dessert tables.

---

49. *Ibid.*, p. 157.

50. *Ibid.*, pp. 160-161.

51. Frances Parke Custis, A Booke of Sweetmeats, No. 7-75.

In all forms of the preserving process it was of first importance to prepare the syrup properly. Even double-refined sugar had to be clarified.[52] For this purpose egg whites beaten to a froth were added to the water and sugar; as the mixture boiled, the egg whites rose to the top along with the dross and made it easier to skim off the black scum; after repeated skimming, the syrup was strained. When it was boiled again, a white scum rose and had to be skimmed off until the syrup was clear. Boiled longer, until it was thicker and the color of strong beer, it was called a full syrup, suitable for preserves. In candy making there were three "heights" to which the syrup could be boiled. The first, called manus Christi height, was reached when it formed a thread. At candy height it formed flakes "like bird lime." At casting height, "the last and greatest height you can boyle your sugar too except you will have it to burne," it flew from the stirring stick "in great flakes like flakes of snow, or like fethers flying in the Ayre."[53]

---

52. Randolph, Virginia Housewife, pp. 154-155, suggests the use of "the pure amber coloured sugar house syrup from the West Indies" because "it never ferments, and the trouble is very much lessened by having ready made syrup, in which it is only necessary to boil the fruit till clear."

53. Custis, Booke of Sweetmeats, No. 1-6.

Firm fruits--cherries, plums, apricots, peaches, pears, pippins--could be "dried" after they had been preserved by taking them from the syrup and placing them on sieves, flat pans, or plates to dry in the sun or in a warm oven. As they dried, more thick syrup was added, a little at a time, and they had to be turned frequently for even crystallization. Some cooks used dry sugar instead of the additional syrup or with it.[54] Peach and apricot chips were made of sliced fruit dried in this fashion, and orange and lemon peel were candied by similar recipes.[55]

Flower petals could be candied in much the same way, but to preserve their colors another process was preferred:

> To Candy rose leaves to look fresh
>
> Take of the fayrest rose leavs red or damask and sprinkle them with rose water & lay them one by one, on white paper on a hot sunshiney day then beat some double refind sugar very small & sift it thinly on the roses, thorough fine laune sive & they will candy as they ly in the hot sun then turne the leaves & strow some rose water on the other side, & sift some sugar in like manner on them, turne them often sometimes strowing on water, & sometimes sifting on sugar till they be enough, then lay

---

54. Smith, Compleat Housewife, pp. 101-102, 122-123; Harrison, Pocket-book, pp. 164-167; Glasse, Art of Cookery, pp. 159, 301, 344, 346-347, 352-353; Raffald, English Housekeeper, pp. 240-245; Randolph, Virginia Housewife, p. 159; Custis, Booke of Sweetmeats, No. 101-105.

55. Custis, Booke of Sweetmeats, No. 93, 94, 99; Randolph, Virginia Housewife, p. 156.

them in boxes betwixt clean papers
& soe keep them all the year.[56]

Gum arabic mixed with the rose water made the petals take

the sugar better and added brilliance to their sparkle.

Candied violets, clove pinks, marigolds, yellow borage,

blue rosemary and succory flowers were equally valued as

colorful confections.[57]

Walnuts and almonds, eryngo and ginger roots, angelica

stalks and roots, marjoram and mint leaves were sometimes

crystallized. Mrs. Custis also chopped or mashed them and

stirred them into a manus Christi syrup, which was dropped

into "rock candies" or "cakes" about the size of a sixpence.

Fruit juices carefully strained produced clear drops and

cakes. The pulp of fruits and berries, treated like the

almond paste in marchpane, made pastes in a great variety

of flavors and colors: apricots, peaches, pears, plums,

quinces, pippins, raspberries, gooseberries, barberries,

cherries, oranges, lemons. Even more decorative was Paste

Royall, printed in molds and then gilded.[58]

Fruit jellies, on the other hand, were less varied

---

56. Custis, Booke of Sweetmeats, No. 81.

57. Ibid., No. 82-88.

58. Ibid., No. 89-92, 97, 98, 111-140. For similar but less explicit recipes see Smith, Compleat Housewife, pp. 104-110, 113-117, 120-124; Glasse, Art of Cookery, pp. 305, 307, 333, 359; Raffald, English House-keeper, pp. 237-247.

than modern ones, and their use was limited to desserts.
Only currants and quinces contained enough pectin to jell
properly; other flavors had to be fortified with currants
or the isinglass or hartshorn shavings used in elaborate
made dishes.[59]

Thus with salt, sand, and sugar the colonial housewife was able to provide supplements to her fresh food
supplies. Her accent on meat and bread and sweets, especially in winter menus, is understandable to modern cooks
because of the limited number of preservatives available
to her. Impressed with her efforts to balance the arrangement of dishes on her table, we are struck with the absence
of any effort to balance her family's diet. She was a complete stranger to principles of sanitation and nutrition
because disease germs would wait another century to be discovered and the nutritional deficiencies of plentiful, appetizing food would not be understood until our own time.
She knew only that fresh food, prepared and served with attention to cleanliness, tasted better and was more easily
digested. Guided by taste and experience, she practiced an
art--not a science.

---

59. Randolph, Virginia Housewife, p. 158; Custis,
Booke of Sweetmeats, No. 210-219; Raffald, English House-
keeper, p. 210.

INDEX